IT TAKES BALLS

IT TAKES BALLS

*Dating Single Moms and Other Confessions
from an Unprepared Single Dad*

JOSH WOLF

GRAND CENTRAL
PUBLISHING

NEW YORK   BOSTON

Grand Central Publishing
Hachette Book Group
237 Park Avenue
New York, NY 10017

www.HachetteBookGroup.com

Printed in the United States of America

RRD-C

First Edition: March 2013

10 9 8 7 6 5 4 3 2 1

Grand Central Publishing is a division of Hachette Book Group, Inc. The Grand Central Publishing name and logo is a trademark of Hachette Book Group, Inc.

The Hachette Speakers Bureau provides a wide range of authors for speaking events. To find out more, go to www.hachettespeakersbureau.com or call (866) 376-6591.

The publisher is not responsible for websites (or their content) that are not owned by the publisher.

Library of Congress Control Number: 2012956254

To Trevor, Kaitlynn, and Jacob.
Without you three, none of
these stories would be possible.
And to Beth, I love you, stupid.
Thank you for making me whole.

Contents

IT TAKES BALLS

CHAPTER 1

Single Mothers

S ingle mothers are pretty damn good in bed.
   You heard me.

Pretty. Damn. Good.

I mean, it makes sense, doesn't it? They've been cooped up in a house with kids all day, having no grownup discussions, sometimes not even speaking in full sentences, making lunches, doing homework, going shopping… basically doing everything. So, when they finally put the kids asleep and have a few hours before they pass out completely exhausted, they are ready to release some pent-up frustration.

Let me introduce myself. My name is Pent-Up Frustration. Pleased to meet you.

Or it was anyway. I went through a period there where the only people I was dating were single moms. Hell, I was a single father, so it made sense but the problem was that I was still young enough where I didn't want to just date breeders. As a matter of fact, I was actively trying to stay away from people with kids, but it just wasn't possible. The girls my age wanted nothing to do with a single guy with three hangers-on. Shocker. But the moms? A single dad, who was a little bit broken but still responsible enough to take care of three kids by himself? It made those women looser than if they'd had two Vicodin and a Soma. The one thing I learned fast about single moms was that because of drama with their ex, kids' schedules, and life, getting involved with them was a roller coaster with lots of rules and regulations. Sex, however, was always good and they were always up for a roll around as long as it fit into the schedule. I remember one woman who told me to be at her house at 9:10 because she put the kids down at 8:45. I would walk in, and she literally had a comforter down on the floor no more than five feet away from the front door. She said there was no need for me to go any farther into her home. She lined up three bottles of water by the comforter so I didn't have to go into the kitchen and there was a bathroom five feet from our makeshift love nest. She wanted to be in bed with the lights out by 10:15. No talking wanted, and cuddling was not an option. It was truly romance at its finest. Not gonna lie, she scared me a little.

Not gonna lie, I also liked it. I liked it a lot.

It was really an interesting experience for me being a single dad. At first, I had no idea what would happen or if I would ever get laid again. All I could think about was who in the world wants to sleep with a wannabe comedian with no job and three kids? Turns out, more people than I thought; they just weren't the people I was thinking of. I remember the first day I showed up to school after my ex and I split. It was hilarious. When I was with my ex, I would show up to school in the morning and all of the women were in sweatpants, no makeup, hair all jacked up—you know, the way people look in the morning when they roll out of bed and throw something on. Right after my ex and I split up, I showed up to school and I didn't recognize a bunch of the women because their makeup was perfect, their hair was teased and blow-dried, and they all looked like they were dressed to go out for a drink. Who were those women, you ask? The single moms. It was insane. For the first time in my life, I was being pursued in a big way and it was pretty freakin' awesome.

"I heard the news. I am so sorry. Do you want to go out for coffee and talk about it?"

And...

"It's just so sad. I've been through exactly what you're going through. What you need is a nice home-cooked meal."

And...

"My door is always open for you. I mean that. Always open...day or night."

It was crazy. I felt like a free agent baseball player who everyone wanted on their team. There was one particular woman who was absolutely insane. She was a very attractive black woman, who was always drunk. Always. She read to our kids' kindergarten class one day completely hammered. She was reading, " 'One fish, two fish, red fish, blue fish' " and slurred her way through all of it. The best part is that she gave a running drunk commentary as she read the book. She'd say things like, " 'Here are some who like to run. They run for fun in the hot, hot sun.' Ugh. Run in the sun? Who does that shit? You get all swampy." Her ex-husband was some bigwig, so she had tons of dough and absolutely no reason to ever work or do anything productive. She literally, no exaggeration, would see women talking to me (this is at 8 AM, mind you), walk up, grab my Johnson, and say things like, "You ready for this black bitch?"

Huh?

Don't get me wrong, I was really fuckin' turned on by it, and that worked every time she did it, but the frenzy was something I couldn't understand. When I was single without kids, I didn't have near this amount of success. Not even close. But now, no job, no money, driving a minivan with three kids in the back, I get rich chicks walking up to me and grabbing my dick at an elementary school. It didn't make any sense. For some of those ladies, when I drove up to school with three kids in the back of my Toyota Sienna I could almost hear vaginas starting to hum. (Not sure what that means exactly but I sure enjoyed writing it.) It was time to readjust my game and try to get out there.

I don't want you thinking that I started sleeping with tons of women right when my ex and I broke up. I mean, I did, but it's not like our break-up was a shock to me, her, or anyone within one hundred miles of us. Our relationship had run its course long before we actually broke up so the actual split was just a formality. I think one of the reasons I stayed in the relationship for so long was that I didn't think there was any way in hell that anyone else would go out with me (see above reasons). The other reason was that I was scared out of my fucking mind to raise three kids by myself. I still felt like a kid myself. Shit, I still jerked off into a sock. People who masturbate into socks shouldn't be in charge of other people's lives.

Getting back out there was going to be a challenge for myriad reasons. I know some of you are thinking, "There must have been some times when you didn't have to go out with a parent, right? There had to be some young'un who was willing to share the wealth." Nope. I had some serious limitations that made me have to find creative ways to work around them and that meant I had to start living by a few rules myself.

Rule number one: There clearly wasn't going to be any sex happening at my place. My kids and I all lived in a one-bedroom. Not that easy to bring a girl back to my place and be like, "(Whispering) Don't worry about them. They're real heavy sleepers. Wait…where are you going? Don't go!" Not only was there no room, but I had decided I wasn't going to introduce my kids to anyone who I didn't think was going to be in their lives for a long time. On top of that, my apartment was a fucking disaster. It's so funny that apartments all over the country have these fancy, exotic-sounding names like Shangri La Apartments or Hollywood Treasure and inside they look like a place where people get murdered for crack. My place was no different and it was called The Luxury Apartments. Not gonna get a lot of va-jay-jay when you open the door to your place and it looks like a fucking sweatshop. There were kids crammed on the floor of my bedroom and clothes and toys thrown all over like an aisle at Marshalls. There was no way anyone would fuck me in that place, and if someone would have, it would have been very clear that that person had some serious problems.

Rule number two: I couldn't do anything that cost

money because I had no more than $200 in my bank at any time and paid the bills catering Mexican food three times a week. I smelled like goat cheese quesadillas for two years of my life. I know this is going to sound like a statement made by Captain Obvious but having no money really limits what you can do. I hear people say they have no money, but I literally had nothing. I seriously could not afford to take someone to the movies. So the question then becomes, what else do you do? There are only so many times that someone will go hiking with you. Especially if you start insinuating that it might not be a bad place to visit later that night. (See Rule Number One to figure out why I was looking for an outdoor spot to have sex.) There are only so many times you can ask a girl out on a picnic. Ugh. Just typing that brings back memories that make my fucking skin crawl. I was always the guy who made fun of people and their picnics. "Oh, so sorry. Did my ball knock over your red plastic cups that you brought out for your ridiculous fucking picnic?" There was something so emasculating about them. And uncomfortable. Holy shit. The worst. The absolute fucking worst. I had to do it though because it was easily disguised as romantic and thoughtful. Also, another place to insinuate we should go back to later that night. (Again, see Rule Number One.) I actually did get a girl to meet me back at the picnic spot for some outdoor sex one night. Couldn't believe it. At the picnic, she had said, "This is really romantic. I love picnics. I also really like lying on a blanket and looking at the stars."

Uh...me, too. I like that, too.

We decided to meet later that night. Same spot. I was bringing the blanket and she was bringing the vagina. I don't think that's exactly what we said when we made the plans but I'm pretty sure it was understood. I got there before she did to clean out the ground underneath the blanket. The last thing I wanted was a stick or a rock jabbing either one of us in the ass or leg and derailing the fun train. I also wanted to make sure we weren't too visible. I desperately wanted to get laid but I couldn't get arrested for it. That would have been no bueno. She showed up wearing a sweater, a pair of jeans, and carrying a bottle of wine. Personally, I would have gone with a skirt if I were her because the skirt never really needs to come off and if shit goes down you want to be able to get up and get out of there in a hurry. But different strokes for different folks, right? We open the wine, start talking, look at the stars for a little while, and, when enough time has passed so I don't feel like a degenerate for making a move on her...I make a move on her.

Boy, did I ever read those signs wrong. Ouchy.

Turns out, she was wearing jeans because it never even crossed her mind that she would be taking them off. "Did you think we were going to have sex? Outside?" (Yes. Yes, I did.*)

"I'm a grown woman. Why on earth would you try to have sex with me for the first time outside on a blanket that looks like it's been sitting in the back of your car for two years?" (It was one year and that's exactly where I got it.)

Then she said, "The least you could have done was to bring me back to your place and try it."

(*Obviously, she wasn't that well versed on Rule Number One.)

Rule Number Three: On top of that, when I made a date, I couldn't pick them up; I had to meet them there. I usually didn't tell people right away that I had kids and, even if I did, I never, ever muttered the word "minivan." The word "van" by itself is horrible. "Hey, wanna take a ride in my van?" Nope, never good. It sounds pretty rapey, actually. Now try adding the word "mini" in front of it. "Hey, wanna take a ride in my minivan?" I'm sure just reading it there are ovaries drying up all around the country.

So, I had no money to take people out, and I had nowhere to take them back to when I did take them out and, on top of that, they had to find their own way to and from whatever free places we were going to. I think it goes without saying that I got a lot of work done over that period of time.

I was completely frustrated because I was fighting my

fate. There was no way around the fact that I had three kids. There was also no way around the fact that I was a horny dude who wanted to have boobies in my face. Then it happened. One day, a whole new world opened up. A world that was right in front of me the entire time. I was at the park one day when my youngest was about three years old. I had him on the swing and I looked over to see this row, I mean *row*, of good-looking Hispanic nannies.

Hola.

One of the nannies, who had to be about twenty-four years old or so, was definitely checking me out, so I held Jacob on the swing a couple of times in a few poses that for sure showcased the guns.

Glanced over... still looking. Game on.

I walk over to the row of women, started chatting them up, and as soon as they heard I was a single dad the whole tone changed. "Oh, what a great guy!" "Do you need help?" and blah, blah, blah. I could *feel* the difference with my little hot mamacita. I mean, as soon as she heard I was a single dad, it was like her temperature changed. Nannies? How come I had never thought of that before? We all talked a little longer until the ladies had to get the kids back to their houses for a nap. And that's when I heard, "Do you want to bring Jacob and have lunch with us at the house?" But it was said with a sexy Hispanic accent that is very hard to type.

Holy shit. I mean, this really applied all three of my rules: not my house, no money, and, honestly, who the fuck cares if I was driving a minivan because she was too! Nanny sex happened that very afternoon. Also that afternoon was when the "shift" started. Let's not think of who won't have sex with me because of those three rules; let's think of who will.

Who else might not want anyone in their messy-clothes-everywhere, sippy-cup-stained-diaper-smelling, too-tired-to-get-up-and-clean-a-fucking-thing apartment? Single moms.

Who might not have the extra money to go out to a $200 dinner because they have to pay for day care, diapers, dentists, and heavy medication just to stay sane? Single moms.

And who, out of anyone in the world, not only wouldn't run *from* but might run *into* a minivan? Single moms.

And then it really hit me. Wait a second, I have to completely change my eye level here. I don't have to hide the kids to pick up women...I have to flaunt them. It was like bringing a puppy and a keg to the beach. I was instantly likeable and they attracted women. I know it sounds like I had decided to use my kids to pick up women, because that's exactly what I did. To be fair to myself, I never did it in a way that put them in danger or where they were being ignored or neglected. I did things like one day I was in the supermarket with my youngest son and we were in the fruit section doing a thing where he would pick up pieces of fruit and toss them in the air for me to catch in one of those little plastic bag thingies. It was our favorite thing to do in the supermarket and, apparently, it was also adorable, because when I looked up I saw a gorgeous woman smiling at us.

I said to my son, "Do you wanna play a different game?"

"Sure."

"Okay, you pick a name you want me to call you, any name at all, and that's what I have to call you for the rest of the day."

"Hmmm. Okay, I want you to call me Snake Guy! Snake Guy!"

Snake Guy? Worst name ever.

"My turn," I said.

"Okay, go."

"I want you to call me 'uncle.' Deal?"

"Deal."

And I walked over and talked to that cute girl. Questionable? Sure. Borderline wrong? Yup. Did desperate times call for desperate measures? You bet your sweet ass they did. He did great, by the way. He called me "uncle" the whole time. Brings a tear to my eye just thinking about it. Natural-born wingman, that kid.

I found out that there was a whole unexplored world

out there that nobody was tapping into: Single Mommy Land. It was like Atlantis. You just had to know where to look to find it. Where could I go—that didn't cost me any money—to run into these elusive creatures? At first, it was like hunting Sasquatch because my eyes weren't trained to see them. In the past, I had ignored the flustered-looking woman who was wearing sweatpants in the supermarket and looking at a list, while shuffling through a pocket full of coupons. I would never look up to see the exhausted-looking women at the park, who sat in the shade with books, looking like they hadn't been off their feet since the beginning of time. I hadn't seen them because I hadn't wanted to.

The park turned into my nightclub. Seriously, I was like a regular who walks into a bar and gets greeted by all of the other alcoholics who hang out there every night. Picking up a woman at the park is really no different than picking up a woman at a bar. Wait, I just read that last sentence and I take it back. It is a little harder because nobody is shitfaced and ready to go bang in the backseat of your car. Also, at the park, nobody goes there thinking, "I think I might get laid." Nobody except me, that is. I was just playing the cards that I had been dealt, my friends. Don't judge. There was always a way to manipulate your time there that would shine you in the best light. What I learned fast is that if you're the guy who has all of the kids chasing him or is in charge of pushing the swings or is basically doing anything where you are engaging with a large group of children, there's a good possibility that you could see a vagina that night. All I had to do was play a game of "chase" and I was good to go. I just had a group of kids run after me and then after about ten minutes, fall down on the ground so they could all jump on top of me and it was a guarantee. The only problem with that game was that about fifty percent of the time I ended up getting hit in the nuts.

The other good move at the park involved "showcasing" my own kids. This was a little more complicated because, well, my kids obviously had no idea that I was trying to meet women so I don't wanna say they cock blocked me but...sometimes they kinda cock blocked me. Things would be going well and they would get tired or act out. Or one time, when he was three, my son really screwed things up. I was talking to this beautiful woman who told me that she had noticed how sweet I was with not only my son but all of the kids on the playground. I told her that I wasn't sure who was having more fun, me or the kids. May I just say, right when those words came out of my mouth I was thinking, "Holy shit, that's a good line. Don't forget to say that one again." We talked for about ten more minutes before she asked if my son and I wanted to head to her house for lunch. Uh...yes. Jacob was playing on the monkey bars with some other kids, so I called him over to tell him we were taking off for lunch. He ran over to me and I said, "Hey buddy, guess what?"

"You want me to call you Uncle again?"

Well, fuck. That is the one drawback to having a four-year-old wingman: no etiquette. Needless to say we didn't go back to her house for lunch.

Those instances were few and far between because most of the time when I was "showcasing" my kids, I figured out a place for both of us to shine. And on some days it came together like magic. I remember one day I was swinging Jacob on the swings when this guy, about my age, walks up and puts his son in the swing next to Jacob. Besides talking to women at the park, there was another major component to my daily trips, and that was competition. I know this sounds incredibly childish—it is and I don't give a shit—but the truth is, all dads are competitive when it comes to their kids. Don't let anyone tell you differently. I know some of them will say, "It's just important to me that Billy has a good time" or "As long as Donna has a positive learning experience, that's what really matters." Bullshit. Bullshit, bullshit, bullshit. I don't care if it's Peewee baseball or a regional spelling bee, you want your kid to win. And on top of that, you secretly don't like the kids they're competing against. Oh yeah, next time you're at an event, look out across the sea of fatherly faces and the ones who are cheering their kids on with "Go, Tommy! You can do it!" The ones doing that, what they're really thinking is, "I hope that kid in the red shirt shits the bed." And it's not a malicious thing. It really isn't. It's thousands of years of genetics. The park is a petri dish for that kind of stuff. Fathers are there with their sons. The fruit of their loins. The person who is going to pass on the family name, and by God they are going to pass it on the way we want them to. Yes indeed, it is like that in a big, bad way. I'm no different. I wish I were. I truly do. And it really isn't about the kids; that's the sad thing. It's a crazy pissing match between two guys who are past their prime for anything meaningful and are just trying to eke out one more victory of any kind.

So, one day at the park, this guy puts his son on the swing next to Jacob. I look over, size the kid up, and notice that this guy is doing the same thing to Jacob. We introduce ourselves to be cordial, but we both know it's not about us. From this point on we're basically measuring the size of our dicks by whose kid is better. That's what it comes down to. When we were younger it was who bench-pressed the most, who got the best score on the SATs, who slept with the most women, who could drink the most beer—all cock fights. Well, now that you have a kid, that's the thing. When did they walk, what kind of grades do they get, what college did they get into, how much money do they make—it never ends. So we start pushing our kids and talking. He tells me that he's in the music business and he's really enjoying the scene and—whatever, bro... Let's skip the bullshit, shall we?

"How old is your boy?" I asked.

"Three and a half. Yours?" he replied.

"Three." Jacob was bigger. Yes! Good guys, one. Bad guys, nothing. This was going to be an easy win over this abnormally small child. I almost felt bad until I remembered a win is a win. This also was a day when there were a ton of good-looking moms and nannies at the park. A ton. It was like they were casting for MILF Hunters next to the jungle gym. I had to play this kinda cool. There was a way to beat this guy and still not look like the asshole in front of the people I was hoping to penetrate.

"What's your boy's name?" I asked.

"Amethyst."

There was a brief silence.

"It's his birth stone," he said.

Yikes. Did he want his kid to get beat up in school? Because he sure was going to do a lot of fighting with the name Amethyst. Holy shit. It was obvious that this man was very progressive and had definitely given his wife way too much leeway when it came to naming the kid. I know a lot of fathers almost feel guilty about fighting for a name. Guys who I've talked to have told me that they just didn't feel right because the woman did all of the work. She carried the baby, went through all of the ups and downs of the pregnancy, and they really thought that if it was between what she wanted and what he wanted, she should have the final say. I definitely don't have an argument for that, but I do have an argument for naming your kid fucking Amethyst! Or any other rock for that matter. While we're at it, I think months of the year should be out of the question; places and any first name that rhymes or matches the last name (I knew a Brian O'Brien and a Neil McNeil) should be outlawed also. It's hard enough being a kid; you don't need people making fun of you right at attendance. I know people say, "It's the person who makes the name" and I would generally agree with that except if you are young boy and your name is Amethyst. He is going to be teased, bullied, and pushed to the point where he will either retreat into a shell or invent some sort of software that turns him into Iron Man, or at some point he will explode into a homicidal rage and we'll all read about him in the papers. The neighbors will all say, "He was such a quiet boy and they seemed to be such good parents." Yeah, except for the fact that they named him Amethyst.

I digress. I told him that my son's name was Jacob and he just nodded, knowing that he was going to lose the name battle almost every time he hits the playground. It

18

was 2-0 and it could be a shutout. "Does your son go to school?" he asked.

"He goes to preschool but he's a little young for school," I said.

"Yeah, most kids his age are still in a preschool. It's just that Amethyst's been reading for a year so I wasn't sure what Jacob was doing." *Bam!* I walked right into that one. Like a good fighter he had lured me into his strength. So, Amethyst is a scholar of sorts. Not too surprising really. I mean with the name-size combo he was working with, he better be smart. Now, 2-1 and I could see that I was in for a bit of a fight. As we continued to compete, the score got to be 4-4 and I was in panic mode. I was used to Jacob crushing kids in these competitions. His size and personality were really hard to overcome. But intellect—we hadn't come up against that yet. Jacob was a lot of things: cute, happy, tall, and coordinated, but a whiz kid? Not so much. We had never battled a scholar before and it was making me nervous.

Usually, after one of these pissing matches, I would glide over to one of the nannies or single moms hanging around the park and say something like, "Why does it always have to be a competition?" The ladies would agree and shake their heads. I would go on to tell them about the other father who was comparing his child to Jacob and how all children were different, which is something to be embraced. It was all part of the plan. You should have seen it. When it worked, it really was a thing of beauty. This was not one of those times. My competitive juices were overriding the horny ones and I had completely put my penis out of my mind. I wanted to win.

We were tied up 4-4 and with every question-answer repartee, we pushed our kids a little harder on the swing. Not only that, we basically just started lying.

"Jacob can name every player on the Red Sox."

"Yeah? Well, Amethyst knows his U.S. states and capitals."

And we pushed them higher. "Amethyst learned Spanish from the nanny." Push.

"Well, Jacob eats the hot sauce at Taco Bell." Whoosh!

At one point, I looked up, and when I tell you that these kids were flying, these kids were flying. And then something happened that changed the game. Something happened that should have made both of us reassess what the fuck we were doing to begin with.

Amethyst started to cry.

A crying baby at the park is like someone screaming "Immigration!" at a soccer game; it gets people's attention. And by "people," I mean the moms and nannies. I looked over and they were all staring at the two of us. If I ever wanted to play hide the diaper with any of the women watching, I had to plan my exit strategy and fast.

There were basically two options at this point. The bigger man would have taken his son off the swings, apologized for being so immature, and walked away. I, however, am not the bigger man and went for option number two. I turned to the guy and said, "What's the matter? Is your son scared?" Looking back, I wish I had been the bigger man because this guy reached back and ... *launched* his kid! I mean ... Houston, we have a problem ... because he just sent his kid into outer fucking space. Launched. You remember when you used to swing and you hit that point way up in the air where the chain on the side bent and you were almost floating? And then ... Wham! It slammed you back down! That's what happened to this kid. I saw it coming, so I immediately grabbed Jacob, took him off the swings, and walked in the direction of the women who were now watching in disgust. Right before I got to them, I turned back to the guy and said with contempt, "What's up with you, bro?" Turned right back to the ladies and said, "Why does it always have to be a competition with these guys?"

It was a game that changed daily and since the same women were at the park every day, you had to be tricky. The problem with the nannies, I found out, was that they all talked to each other, so once you rolled around with one of them, you had to go to another park.

Moms weren't like that at all. They actually would say things like, "I don't want this getting around school so you can't tell anyone." Perfect. The biggest problem I had with trying to arrange for sex with single moms is that both of our households had kids in them. That made time and circumstance incredibly important. I was lucky enough to have my brother and a few friends who were willing to bite the bullet and watch my kids for a few hours while I kept my sanity. Most women, like my friend who threw the blanket down on the floor, just told me to come over after the kids went to sleep. Usually, it worked like a charm. Usually. There was one time when I was having sex with this woman and I felt this finger touch my ass. My first thought was, "Holy shit, this chick's a magician." Until I turned around and saw her four-year-old son staring at me.

Noooooooooooooooooooooo!!!!!!!!!!!!!!

I had no idea what to do. This tiny little boy was at the foot of the bed, half asleep, just rubbing his eyes and there I was butt-ass naked and banging his mom. Ugh. If you're reading this right now, buddy, I am so sorry. Well, not that sorry but sorry enough. So, there I was, boner out (his mother was hiding under the covers by the way, saying, "Just don't move. He'll go away. Don't move." What was he, a fucking T-Rex?) with this little child looking at me and all I could think to do? Pull the Jedi mind trick on him. I know how incredibly stupid that sounds but it was the only thing I could think of! First, most of the blood in my body was not in my brain at that time, and second, I just really wanted to go back to having sex with this kid's mom so I was willing to try anything.

I looked at him straight in the face and said, "Jason, you're sleeping. Go back to your room. You're sleeping. You're mommy's sleeping. Everyone's sleeping." He stared at me for a beat, blinked, and walked back into his room. I couldn't believe it worked. Having sex and being a Jedi in the same night? I think eight nerds' heads just exploded reading that. Unfortunately, I did not get to finish the job. I don't know why. She said something about seeing her kid took her out of the "mood."

What is this "mood" women talk about? You know what my "mood" is? Breathing. "I have to be in the mood." Yeah? Well, I have to be awake. Wait a minute, wait a minute. That's not true either because sometimes you can finish the job asleep. That always shocked me. I mean, how horny do you have to be to be knocked out and still have an orgasm?

I did stumble across some pretty interesting women who were into some pretty weird shit. There was one woman I went out with who only wanted to have sex in the minivan. She loved it. Never asked why, and to tell you the truth, I never really cared. All I knew was that when she called, I would go to her house, we would kiss for a bit, and then she'd ask me if I wanted to "hit the van." The first time she asked me that I couldn't believe what I was hearing. She wanted to leave the comforts of her home to go knock it out on the street in my van.

There was one woman who called me every once in a while and only wanted me to take her places that she and her ex-husband used to go to. She would spend most of the night bitching about how worthless he was, get herself all worked up, and then we would go back to her house and have some pretty aggressive, angry sex. The best part? She would always give me something of his when I left. I actually met the guy once at a school function and he commented on the fact that he had a shirt "just like" the one I was wearing.

Oops.

I think the weirdest situation I ever found myself in was with this single mom who also was training to be a body builder. Let me just say that I don't really have a "type." I've dated all colors, creeds, shapes, and sizes. For me, I've always had the attitude of "How do I know I don't like it if I've never tried it before?" I really challenged that motto with this woman because I never thought I would date someone with bigger biceps than me. I met her at the gym one day and I couldn't stop staring at her. Besides the fact that she really did have a beautiful face, I had just never seen a woman so muscular before. We started talking and I found out that she was a single mom who was training for one of the Southern California body-building competitions. At first, she was going to join the fitness part of the competition because she was scared about getting too muscular, but after lifting heavy for a few months, she said she really got addicted to it and decided to give it a try.

I have to admit that I barely heard a word she was saying because I was just staring at her body. Her pecs (that's what they were, pecs—not boobs) were ripped, her arms were massive, and I was pretty sure her legs could crush me like an empty Pepsi can. I couldn't tell if I was scared or turned on. Before I could decide, she told me her name was Jenna and asked me if I wanted to go out for a drink some time, and I said sure. I hadn't had a woman ask me out like that in a long time. When I got back to my apartment, there was a message on my machine from her just saying how nice it was to meet me and that she was looking forward to our drink together. We spoke a few times on the phone that week and it was always her calling me. She would ask me about what I did with my day and was always extra complimentary about everything. It was a completely different dynamic than I had ever had with a woman before and I kinda liked it.

The night of the date, we went to a bar in Hollywood and things were going really well. She wasn't that funny, which is usually a huge deal breaker for me, but she was more attentive than any woman I had ever been out with.

If my drink needed more ice, she would make sure I had it. If my cocktail napkin got too wet, she would make sure I had a dry one. When I told a joke that I knew wasn't very funny, she gave it an extra hard laugh. Honestly, it was a pretty good feeling and then...things got a little weird. We were sitting in a booth and some guy who was walking by spilled his drink on me. Before I could say anything, I heard, "Hey! Watch where you're going!" I turned and Jenna was already out of the booth and in this guy's face. Neither I nor the guy knew what to do.

"Excuse me?" he asked.

"I said watch where you're going. Now, apologize to my friend and keep walking," she said.

"Jenna, I can handle this. You really don't have to—"

"Are you going to apologize to my friend or not?" she said, moving a little closer to the guy.

I couldn't believe what I was a part of. Some dude accidentally spilled his drink on me and *my* date was picking a fight with him? It was completely bizarre. Wait a minute, wait a minute, wait one fucking minute...it was all starting to make sense. The attention, the phone calls, the fake laughs. Holy shit! I was the chick on this date! The guy was clearly as confused as I was because he looked at me, looked back at her, and said, "Uh...yeah. Really sorry I spilled my drink on you, bro. Really was an accident."

I just shrugged my shoulders and said, "Yeah, that's cool. No worries at all, man," and he walked off.

"Do you need a towel or something?" she asked.

"No, thanks," I said, still a little stunned by my realization. Now that I knew my role, I had to decide how the rest of this night was going to play out. There were basically two options: Either I couldn't handle who I was being asked to be that night and I leave, or I embraced it and saw what happened next. The truth is, I didn't mind being coddled for the night. Shit, I knew I couldn't live that way but it wasn't bad, not gonna lie. Also, and I feel a little weird saying it, I felt like I owed her a little roll around. She picked me up, she paid for drinks, she "protected my honor," I figured the least I could do was put out. And, truthfully, I had never been with a girl that muscular and I wanted to see what it was like.

When we got back to her house, she turned on music, made me a drink, and asked me if I wanted a massage. I couldn't believe it! She was using my moves on me! The thing I realized while this was happening was just how transparent guys are. I mean, I knew everything she was doing was part of a grand plan to get me in the sack. I also realized that night that a girl decides way before a guy makes a move if she's going to have sex with him. Being on the other side was eye-opening, to say the least.

We did end up having sex that night, and no, she did

not take out a strap-on, which is what everyone who has ever heard that story has asked. Honestly, I was kinda worried about that myself. We never really hung out after that night. She got pretty busy with her body-building competition and I thought it was only a matter of time before she grew a penis.

The women I hung out with during this time in my life really helped to keep me sane. Not only was the adult interaction needed but it made me realize that I wasn't alone going through the muck. Most important, these women showed me that it was okay to live a full, crazy, kinky-ass life even with three kids in tow.

CHAPTER 2

You Gotta Do Whatcha Gotta Do

I think we can all agree that sometimes life is not a box of chocolates. In fact, a lot of times it more resembles a bag of shit. And I've found that, more often than not, your life is defined by what you do with said bag of shit.

There have been more than a few times in my illustrious and all too unsuccessful career that I've wanted to pack up shop and head home but none more than the period of my life when I was living in a one-bedroom with my three kids. My ex and I had split up and the kids (seven, five, and two) were staying with me probably eighty percent of the time. When we were together, my ex was the one who actually held down the day job. I stayed home with the kids during the day and split my nights between catering and comedy. So when we split up, and I was living like a Jewish immigrant circa 1893, I had to try to figure out a way to not only put food on the table but also keep doing comedy. That meant a few things right off the bat: I had to find a job during the day and I had to find cheap, reliable day care.

Did anyone who has kids just read that last sentence and laugh out loud? For those of you without kids, saying "cheap, reliable day care" is like looking for "fun, non-addictive drugs" or asking for "honest, disease-free hookers." Cheap, reliable day care doesn't exist, and I found that out quickly.

I ended up getting my closest friend, a guy I knew from Seattle, to help me babysit. His name was Joey Diaz and I probably should have known better. I'd never met anyone like Joey before. He was a larger-than-life (personality and stomach) Cuban from New York City who really had an appetite for anything life threw at him. He referred to his criminal record as his résumé, as in, "Josh Wolf [he always refers to me by first and last name, or he calls me Judeo], I don't think I can go to Canada because of my résumé."

He also never gets words or phrases right. One time I told him what he was saying "was just semantics" and he told me, "That's not true. I love the Jews." At my daughter's birthday party, when we still spelled things out around her, he told me that the candy was "in the D-R-A-W."

I said, "The what?"

"The D-R-A-W," he insisted.

"I have no idea what you're talking about."

"The draw. It's in the fucking draw!"

"Oh, the drawer?"

"That's not how I say it."

"That's fine. But we all spell it the same on purpose."

My all-time favorite Joey Diaz story, and there are tons of good ones, is about the first time he took ecstasy. For those of you who have never taken ecstasy, well, what are you waiting for? Joey might have had one or two drug-related things on his résumé so he was no stranger to getting high—he had just never experienced this high. When he asked me if I knew where to get some E because he wanted to give his girlfriend "a stabbing" (that's Joey talk for making love), I made a few calls for him.

His girlfriend was a story in itself. They had been dating for a while but she also had a restraining order against him. You read that correctly. So, Joey went over to her apartment one afternoon very excited about the afternoon's "stabbing." As soon as he got there, he took the ecstasy and he and his girlfriend started going at it. What Joey didn't know was that his girlfriend, after one of their huge screaming matches, had told her neighbors about the restraining order and said that if they ever saw him around they should call the cops.

Right when the drugs started to kick in there was a pounding on the front door. The two lovebirds ignored the knocking until it was followed up by "Police! Open the door!" Uh-oh. For anyone who has ever taken E, you know that as soon as it starts to kick in, especially the first time, there is no slowing down that train. All aboard! Please follow your eyes to the back of your head and enjoy the ride!

Panicked, his girlfriend hopped out of bed and told him to hide. High out of his mind, Joey decided to hide under the bed. Not a horrible decision for most people but most people are not Joey Diaz. Joey has a *huge* belly, so when the police walked into the room, his girlfriend said that "it looked like the bed was breathing."

The police cuffed him, took him down to the county jail, and put him in one of those big cells that have a bunch of people in it who are waiting to get processed. Did I mention that he was tripping balls for the very first time? Here is my favorite quote from him about the day: "Josh Wolf, I was in that cell with guys who had been arrested for who knows what and all I could think about is how to ask one of them to rub my back."

I know some of you may be questioning my choice of Joey as my babysitter and I can totally understand that. Truth is, Joey would have stood in front of a bus for my kids and that was the most important thing to me. I've always considered him to be what I would call a moral criminal. He may steal twenty dollars from you, but he'd take you out to lunch with it.

The kids also loved Joey so I didn't really think twice about him babysitting until he came over to my house one day and bent over to pick up a toy that was on the floor.

Joey has never been one for underwear. Enough said.

When he bent over, Kaitlynn (who was six at the time) ripped some hair out of his ass crack and said, "How many?" He shot up and said, "That time it felt like five."

That time? Obviously, it was time to scrap the babysitter idea and figure out how to make money but keep the kids with me.

Times were a little desperate and we definitely did some things as a family that I'm not a hundred percent proud of. For example, we used to eat our lunches and dinners in the aisles at the grocery store. I convinced the kids that it wasn't stealing as long as you ate everything before you left the store. So I would put them in a shopping cart and we would go to the hot food section, make salads, get cookies, and then I would wheel them up and down the aisles until they finished their "meals." To make it entertaining, I would pretend that I was a tour guide and they were tourists, and I would describe the things that they were seeing in the aisles. "Out of the right of the vehicle you'll see what we like to call the diabetes section of the store."

I think my favorite scam we ever ran as a family was at Disneyland. We had gotten some free tickets from a friend and drove down there on what turned out to be the hottest day in the history of the planet earth. It was brutal.

I definitely have no idea why they call it "the happiest place on earth." If anything, it was more like a fucking hostage situation. When I was walking in, a dude was walking by with his family and he looked at me like "Save yourself!" I should have paid attention.

To start off, I knew that prices for everything there were astronomical but eight bucks for a bottle of water? Really? Does that come with vodka and ice? On top of that, the kids started chanting about chili that was served in a bread bowl. They could not fathom how the elves behind the scenes made that happen so of course we had to get a couple of those. Add that to the death heat and crazy lines that were all over the park and I could tell I was not going to last long.

As a Jew, I already have a natural, healthy dislike for standing in long lines and waiting to get on some tram or train. Every line we stood in was at least an hour wait, and having three young kids with no concept of patience just added to my fervent belief that prescription pills should be sold at 7-Eleven.

Where I totally lost my mind was at the It's a Small World ride. We had been waiting for about thirty minutes when my oldest told me he had to use the restroom. Are you kidding me? We're almost halfway through the line

34

and he wanted to get out? How young is too young to pee in a bottle? But we got out of line anyway, went to the bathroom, and returned to the end of the line.

Thirty minutes later and almost halfway through the line, my daughter said, "Daddy, I have to go pee."

I finally understood my father on our family trips when he wouldn't pull the car over to let anyone, my mother included, go to the bathroom. I think his strategy was "I'm just gonna keep going and assume that nobody is going to pee in the car." That day at Disneyland, he started to make a lot more sense to me.

As a grownup I knew that it wasn't my daughter's fault that she had to use the restroom and I also knew that because she was only six she couldn't really hold it very well. But the combo of the heat, the ninety-seven trips to the bathroom we had already taken, and the fact that we were now getting back in line for this fucking ride for the third fucking time had me a bit on edge.

About forty-five minutes later, my youngest son (who was still in diapers) shit his pants. And when I say shit his pants, I mean it was one of those baby poops that you can smell from forty yards away. The kind of poop that as a parent you try to ignore but know you can't because everyone in the general vicinity is looking at you like you beat your kids.

I was trying to ignore the stench but the heat and lack of

a breeze were making that impossible so we walked out of line for the third time to go the bathroom. That was three bathroom trips and almost two hours of waiting in line and we still hadn't made it onto the worst ride in the history of man.

When we got back in line, I was ready to kill someone. I saw a guy in a wheelchair roll past everybody to go to the front, and I actually thought, "Lucky bastard."

An hour later, when we finally got to the front, the kids couldn't have cared less. They were ready to go do something else and I was not having that at all. We were riding this ride and we were going to have fun, damn it!

We didn't. It sucked.

After more than four hours at this park and only one ride, I was looking for any excuse to get mad, and wouldn't you know it, I found one. As I was trying to wrangle my three kids through the park, the man in the wheelchair who rolled by me to the front of the It's a Small World line *walked* past me pushing his wheelchair. What the fuck? I turned around, tapped him on the shoulder, and said, "Uh, excuse me, but weren't you handicapped earlier? What's with the wheelchair?"

He said, "If you're in a wheelchair you get to go to the front of the line."

"So you're not disabled?" I asked.

"Nope."

"Where'd you get the wheelchair?"

"They keep them up front," he said and walked off.

I turned back to the kids and said, "Who wants to be handicapped?" And off we went.

It was surprisingly easy to get a wheelchair. I just walked up front, told them that my daughter had twisted her ankle, and we needed a chair. It's a good thing that my little girl is such a stellar actress because when the guy looked at her she was literally rolling on the ground, grabbing her ankle, and crying, "Hurry, Daddy! It hurts so bad." Smelling a lawsuit, they grabbed a wheelchair and got us the fuck out of there as quickly as they could.

Let me say this for the record: With a wheelchair, Disneyland is the best place in the whole world. Wow. No lines. The first car on every ride. I also learned that *a lot* of people in wheelchairs at Disneyland don't need to be. It was a whole underground society that I didn't know existed. I felt honored to be included in the special club and sorry for the poor fools waiting in line. Every time I saw a guy like me with a bundle of kids I wanted to run up, shake him, and scream, "You fool! Go get a wheelchair and be free!" But I didn't. I didn't want to take the chance that someone would catch on to the scam and take my little golden ticket away. Sorry, folks. Every man for himself.

We ended up having a great time at Disney that day. The only bad thing that came from it was for about a year after, every time we would be in a line anywhere my kids would scream, "Make us handicapped, Daddy! Make us handicapped!" I stopped trying to explain that one.

After cheating The Mouse and eating all of my meals at the grocery store, I knew it was time to figure out a way to make some money. But how? I couldn't work at an office all day because I wasn't trained to do anything that would pay me enough to cover day care and living expenses. I was nowhere near the level in the world of comedy that would have put food on the table, and even if I had been, I wouldn't have been able to travel. I was screwed two ways from Tuesday for sure, and then in a flash of genius or haze of weed (still not sure which), I thought of it.

A peanut-butter-and-jelly sandwich delivery service.

It fit everything I needed. I could do the work at home with the kids, take them with me on delivery runs, go to auditions, and hopefully I could make enough money to keep my little family floating. Everyone loves a good PB&J, right? It was gold, Jerry! Gold!

The first thing I needed to do was figure out the menu. I know that sounds a bit stupid, but being from the East Coast I couldn't do a PB&J without offering the option of Fluff. For those of you who don't know, Fluff is whipped marshmallow goodness in a jar and something that goes with peanut butter like being drunk goes with Taco Bell. It's a perfect match.

The thing that made this business unique, though, was that, along with your lunch in a brown bag, I added a note from your mother. When you ordered your food, I asked what type of note you wanted with it. They ranged anywhere from mild ("Have a great day at school! Love, Mom") to spicy ("I found the weed under your bed and it's way better than the shit we get. Bring your girlfriend by later; your dad thinks she's cute. Love, Mom"). People loved the notes, they loved the brown paper bags, and they loved the sandwiches.

What really made us money though was having the kids deliver the food. Most of our business was to office buildings, so I would take them up the elevator, smear some dirt on their faces, and send them into the office. They always got tipped double the bill, sometimes more. It was a genius plan and we kept getting busier and busier. We actually were starting to make some money and then I did something I never allowed myself to do. I dared to dream. If the business kept going the way it was going, including the two hundred percent tips the kids were getting, I could actually, dare I say, get air conditioning for my car. It was needed...badly.

I had bought my car in Seattle, where you don't really need air conditioning, and obviously the car was much cheaper without it. It wasn't until I got to Los Angeles that I realized how critical A/C was.

I thought that if I just rolled down the windows I'd be fine. Uh...wrong. Not only did rolling down the windows make it too loud to hear the stereo or talk to anyone in the car, and not only were there eight pounds of Saint Bernard hair in the car at all times (my dog at the time) so that when the wind kicked up there was a mini hair tornado choking the life out of you. The absolute worst thing was that when you rolled down the windows, it didn't even really cool you off. It was just hot, hairy air being moved around very quickly.

I tried keeping the windows rolled up and blowing the fan. That should have worked, right? Nope. The problem with keeping the windows up was that you needed to bring a change of clothes for when you got out of the car. You were like a burrito getting cooked in a microwave. I could handle quick trips in the car but anything over five minutes was unbearable. Basically, windows up and you looked like you just ran a marathon; windows down and you looked like you had been raped by a poodle.

But now, air conditioning was in our sights and nothing was going to get in our way.

One day, when I was making sandwiches for our first lunch run of the day, there was a knock at my front door. I told my oldest son to answer it and a few seconds later I heard, "Dad! It's for you!"

I walked out of the kitchen and saw a guy in a suit

standing in my doorway looking stunned. I'm not sure if I've explained to you what our apartment looked like but let me put it as plainly and succinctly as possible. It was one of those tiny, cheap-ass places with permanently stained carpets, and this particular one housed me, three kids, my brother, and a Saint Bernard. To say that there was shit all over the place would be a bit of an understatement.

It wasn't the first time an official-looking guy showed up at my door unannounced. About a year earlier, when my ex still lived in the apartment, we had a different visitor who almost wreaked total havoc on our lives.

I was in our bedroom that day when I heard my dog barking like crazy on the balcony. Bud barked for only two reasons: He couldn't get to something he really wanted and he was horny. Which is kinda the same thing, I guess.

Having a horny dog that outweighs you is a little nerve-racking. I used to joke that I was going to wake up one morning with his paw over my mouth and him leaning down saying, "*Shhh.* Just relax. This is only gonna hurt for a sec."

As I walked out of my bedroom to see who my dog wanted to hump, I heard what sounded like hail landing on my balcony. Seeing as I was in Los Angeles and it was eighty degrees and sunny, I found that to be a wee bit odd. I opened the sliding glass door and I saw all of these tiny rocks on my balcony. Before I could step outside, another bunch of tiny rocks came flying down on my dog.

I looked over the side of the balcony and saw a man one floor below in the next building holding a tiny mutt and a handful of pebbles.

"What the fuck are you doing?" I asked politely.

"Your dog is barking at my dog!" he replied douchebaggily. (New word. How do we like it?)

"And your dog is barking at my dog!" (Which he was.) "That's what they do!"

"Well, I want him to stop."

"So you threw rocks at him? If you want my dog to stop barking, take your dog inside or bring him up here so he can hump him. But I'm telling you, if you throw one more rock at my dog, I'm gonna come down there and shove them into your pee hole."

Always a good threat. Anything being put into the pee hole is an extreme ouchy.

In the apartment he went. I didn't think about it again until a week later when there was a knock at my door. I opened the door and saw a man who was in his midforties with gray Jerry Garcia hair and a suit that looked like it didn't fit him twenty years ago when he bought it. He was holding a briefcase in one hand and a piece of paper in the other.

"Hi, my name is Greg Littleton from Child Protective Services. Do you have children living here?"

Before I could answer, all three of my kids, wearing only their underwear, ran by screaming at the top of their lungs.

"I'll take that as a yes," he said.

"I'm sorry, what's this about?" I asked.

"We had a report that there were three young children walking on the ledge of your balcony last week."

That motherfucker. I threatened to clog up his pee hole and he called CPS on me!

"May I come in?"

Anyone with small kids, much less three of them, will tell you that if you're not expecting company the house is a holy fucking mess. We were folding laundry on the couch, there were toys all over the place, dishes were in the sink, and to top it off, when the kids made one more pass through the living room like they were shooting a remake of *Lord of the Flies*, my ex came storming out of the bedroom in *her* underwear.

"Somebody better be dying with all that screaming, and if they aren't they will be soon!"

Uh, honey, meet the man who can take the kids away. Man who can take the kids away, meet my girlfriend who is trying to sleep off a hangover.

After she ran back into the bedroom, put some clothes on, and had the situation explained to her, we all sat down for a little chat at our dining room table. I would have been scared to death but once I sat down and got a look at this guy I saw that he was a fucking mess. Not only was his suit too small but it hadn't been dry-cleaned since his bar mitzvah. He was wearing two different colored socks and his shoes looked like he tied them to the bumper of his car and dragged them along for the drive to this meeting. In my mind, in order for this guy to find someone inept, things would have to be *really* bad. It turns out they were. Not for us … but for him.

"Well, I can see that it must have been some sort of horrible misunderstanding," he said after an hour in the apartment and a litany of ridiculous questions that would never help determine whether or not I let my kids walk on the balcony wall like it was a tightrope. "You must have really upset this guy for him to make that call to us."

Hell yeah, I did. I threatened the security of his pee hole.

"Well, I won't take any more of your time," he said. "I know how hard it is to raise kids."

"How old are your kids?" I asked.

"Fifteen and seventeen, but I don't see them too much anymore."

Huh?

"I left my wife, who was my high school sweetheart,

two years ago for our housekeeper and she doesn't let me really see the kids anymore," he said.

Excuse me?

"It's not that bad really. I mean, my new wife doesn't have any of the hang-ups that my ex had and it's so cool to see the world through the eyes of a twenty-one-year-old woman."

He took off with a nineteen-year-old? The man whose job it is to make sure children are safe ran off with the maid? This was turning into the worst/best story I had ever heard in my entire life. I don't know how train wrecks like this find their way into my life but I am so grateful that they do. Best Child Protective Services agent *ever*! I had no idea what to say to the guy. Congratulations? Great career choice? Do you babysit? I was drawing a blank but it only got better.

He handed us a business card and said, "Well, I'm not going to waste any more of your time. My name and number are on the card if you two ever need anything."

What in God's name could I ever need from him, you ask? Well, he was about to tell me.

"You two should come by our house and have dinner sometime. You seem like really cool people."

Uh...

"I mean, when I said my new wife has no hang-ups I mean she's got *no* hang-ups at all. And she's cute, bro. I think you'd really like her."

45

Holy shit on a stick. By "no hang-ups" this guy meant she banged other dudes. The CPS guy was a swinger!

"Oh, well, okay," I said, staring at the business card like it had the secrets to the pyramids on it so I didn't have to make eye contact with him. "We'll, uh, definitely call if we, uh, if we…" How do you end that sentence? I couldn't figure it out. If we what? If we wanna go to your house so I can pork your maid-wife? If we decide to swing with you and your dirty-ass suit? Thank God my ex was good at breaking uncomfortable silences. She had to be because she caused so many of them herself.

"We'll definitely call you first if we want to get into some freaky shit. Have a great day," she said. And, just like that, he left.

So when this new official-looking guy stood at my front door, the first thing I looked at was his suit. If it was too small and dirty, maybe it was the CPS guy's son coming to finish what his dad couldn't. Nope—suit clean. Had I threatened the health of anyone's pee shoot recently? Nope. Maybe this guy was here to tell me that raising three kids solo and living like a third-world-country Jew was just a joke and he was about to hand me a million dollars!

To make matters worse, the kids were currently putting peanut-butter-and-jelly sandwiches together on the floor while watching *Blues Clues* and I walked out of the kitchen—ready for this?—shirtless with peanut butter all over my hands.

"Uh...Josh Wolf?" the guy said, looking at a piece of paper.

"That's me."

"Uh-huh. Is this, uh, is this the main business address for PB and J's?"

"It is." We were starting to get walk-up business? Awesome.

And that's when the badge came out. "I'm Tony Williams from the health department and I need to ask you a few questions. Can I come in?"

Were they gonna be questions like, "Are your kids really on the floor making the food you're about to deliver?" Because if that was the case, I would pass. Listen, I don't want to make it sound like I hadn't thought of cleanliness. I had. My oldest son was the only one actually touching food and he had been thoroughly scrubbed down. And the kids weren't actually on the floor making the sandwiches. I had laid out newspapers for them to sit on. That doesn't sound much better, does it?

As Mr. Health Department walked in, I realized that my future as the peanut-butter-and-jelly guy was minutes away from ending and my dream of an air-conditioned car was quickly going down the shitter with it.

"Mr. Wolf, we've got a huge problem."

We? Really? Are you the one treating your kids like a bunch of Kathy Lee Gifford's tiny Asian workers?

"You're not in code for anything. First of all, you're not allowed to run restaurants out of your apartment, and that's basically what this is." He paused. You could tell that he had no idea where to begin with the list of offenses but he plodded on.

"You're making the food with your shirt off. Would you eat somewhere where the head chef was shirtless?"

"You never went to pot roast Fridays at my Nana's," I joked.

Nothing.

"You have to shut this down today. Now. Not another order taken, not another order dropped off. Done."

But...I wanted a car with air conditioning. I was tired of looking like a Wookie when I stepped out of my car. *We needed air conditioning!* For the love of all that's holy, don't take that away from us! Please!

"Shut down? But this is my only source of income. What can I do to make this work?"

"Well, you could start by telling your workers to stop licking their fingers when they get peanut butter on them."

I could see that this was going to be an uphill battle so I pleaded with him man-to-man.

"Listen," I said. "Do you have any idea how hard it is raising three kids by yourself? I'm trying to do the right thing here and I'm trying to do it the right way. I'm not selling drugs, I'm not hurting anyone, and, the truth is, we're really just trying to save enough money to get some air conditioning for my car. The kids are five minutes away from heat stroke every time we have to go to the grocery store. I swear I'll clean this place up. I'll have a maid come in every morning and make sure it's spotless. The kids will have nothing to do with the lunches and I'll make sure that I have a shirt on as soon as I wake up in the morning. You can stop by anytime to make sure it's up to par and if it's not you can shut us down. But you can't shut us down right now. You just can't."

Of course that was all a lie. Do you think that if I could have afforded a maid every day I would have been selling fucking peanut-butter-and-jelly sandwiches for a living? But I thought I had him. I really did. And then my dog shit on the rug. Not a regular dog poop but poop coming from the ass of a Saint Bernard.

Needless to say, under threat of fines and possible jail time, we were shut down that day.

I was left with a lot of disappointed customers and more PB&J inventory than I knew what to do with. Until we got shut down, I had no idea how much people liked seeing the three kids walk into their office to deliver lunch. For me they were the moneymakers, but for a lot of folks stuck in cubicles nine hours a day, three cute, dirt-smeared kids was just the break in the day they needed. Who knew?

The inventory was a real problem. I had just bought stuff for the week so I was totally loaded up and, since at the time I never made enough money to even think about keeping receipts, I couldn't return it.

Lucky for me, about a week later, a good friend of mine came to the rescue. She was working at an agency that was putting on a showcase at the Improv and she wanted to know if I could make four hundred PB&J lunches for the people attending. Hell yeah, I could.

If you're wondering what four hundred PB&Js spread all over a tiny apartment smells like, I'll tell you—air conditioning.

I got calls for sandwiches for about six months after we closed and I still run into people in Hollywood who refer to me as the Peanut Butter and Jelly Guy. It could be worse. They could call me the guy who steals from grocery stores or makes his kids sit in wheelchairs to avoid lines.

P.S. They really should do something to make the kids' rides at Disneyland more enjoyable for the parents who have to ride on them also. "But your joy is supposed to come from seeing the smile on your child's face," we're told. Go fuck yourself. I see that face every day. What's in it for me? How about a TV with ESPN on it? Hook a brother up! And maybe for the women, a mani-pedi given by little elves?

P.P.S. I now understand a lot of things my parents did a whole lot more than I used to. Like when my dad was watching TV in the other room and we were being really loud, he would scream, "Don't make me come in there!" I now know that means, "I don't want to get up!"

How about this one? Do you know that when your parents yelled at you or disciplined you, after they shut the door to your room, at least half the time they started laughing? "Did you see the look on his face when you started yelling? Hysterical!"

Here's another good one. And this one threw me for a bit of a loop when I realized it. As a father, I probably said something today that will have a profound effect on one of my kids for the rest of their lives...and I have no idea what it is. Crazy, right? You think you have all of these great heart-to-heart talks where you share the secret to life and unlock the clues to their future, and all they remember is that you referred to their skinny jeans as "retarded," which leads to fifteen years of therapy.

When you're a young kid, you really think your parents know everything and, truth is, we don't know shit. I pity the first kid. Because it's the parents' first time too. That's why the youngest of a large family always gets away with more. I know that's what happened with me. By the time I was a teenager, my parents' philosophy was, Well, you're not going to listen to anything we say anyway, so just don't die, son.

They had already smelled the weed on clothes and heard the "My eyes are red because Kevin has cats at his house" excuse, caught people sneaking out of and into windows, heard girls throwing late-night rocks, figured out they needed to hide car keys at night, figured out that somebody had made a second set of car keys, listened too many times to "I don't know why I'm throwing up. I must have eaten some bad food," realized that someone replaced their whiskey with apple juice, and been hit with "I don't know why they marked me absent. They must not have seen me in class."

They were tired. Too tired to call us on every lie we told.

Parents start out militant about it. My favorite thing to say to one of my kids is, "You wanna stick with that story or come back later with another one?" You try to bust your kids for every lie. Tell them that the one thing you will not tolerate in your house is lying. I guarantee you that is a quote from every household in the country, but guess what. It doesn't stick. How could it? You're a boxer in the ring with younger, faster opponents and they just keep throwing punches at you. In the first few rounds you do okay, but as the fight wears on, you can't move your head around as much and you're getting really tired. You try to keep up but soon it's clear who's going to win this fight and it sure as hell ain't your tired old ass.

I can't tell you how many conversations my wife and I have had with the kids and after they walk away one of us will say, "Did you believe a word he said?"

Note to teenagers: You are not smarter than us. We just stop caring as much.

CHAPTER 3

Crushed and Flushed

I want to have a baby."

Outside of "I do not give blow jobs," those might be the six words that could change a relationship more than any others. I remember when my wife (I'm married now, FYI) told me about her idea and I couldn't believe what I was hearing. She had already walked into a crazy situation and she wanted to make it crazier?

I already had three kids when we met. The youngest is now thirteen, which means we would be free and clear in five years! Five years! In five years we could walk around the house naked (although in five years, I'm not sure that's gonna be the best idea for anyone). In five years we could go wherever we wanted whenever we wanted. In five years I wouldn't have to spend my Saturdays pretending to cheer other people's kids on when I really only gave a shit about watching my son hit. In five years I would never have to sit through another *painful* school play that made me want to scream "Fire!" and imagine setting one so nobody ever would perform at that school again. In five years we could finally sleep. In five years we would be free.

And she wanted to throw that away for what? Midnight feedings and diaper duty? Uh, I think I'm gonna have to pass. Some backstory might be helpful for everyone so I don't seem like such an asshole.

A long, long time ago I lived in Seattle. Back in the days of flannel and guys with long, squirrel-looking ponytails. I had both, by the way. I had decided to move up there to start my stand-up career because I had heard Los Angeles was full of douchebags and New York is where the Yankees live.

I know, I know, I'm a grown man and a baseball team shouldn't determine where I live or don't live but I hate the Yankees. Hate-hate. Like a hate that burns so strong I had to ask my parents if I was ever "touched" by a babysitter wearing a Yankees hat. So the idea of living in New York with all those Yankee fans was not even an option.

Seattle had a lot of stage time available and was also far, far away from a girl who had just got through crushing and flushing my heart. I figured my moving would show her. I'd get away as far as I could and she'd see for sure that I was over her. Then she'd want me back and I'd tell her, "I'm sorry but I'm over you" and then she'd *beg* me to take her back and I'd say, "Sorry, you had your chance. I'm over you. See? I'm moving to Seattle. How could I not be over you if I'm moving to Seattle?" And then she would cry and cry and cry and I'd say, "Okay. I'll take you back, but this time, if you go down on someone else it's over forever!" I moved to Seattle, and needless to say, nothing in the above mentioned fantasy came close to happening.

You ever think that you might run into someone famous and so you map out the whole conversation in your head? You think about the funny little things you're gonna say and all the questions you'll ask that will really show you're a true fan and not one of those other people. That's what I did, because the house I rented was only eight houses down from where Kurt Cobain lived. I hatched a plan to show Kurt that he and I should hang for sure. I figured I'd see him out sometime when I was walking my dog and I'd see some other people asking him for autographs and stuff and after they finally walked away I'd say something like, "Don't you hate that?" He'd immediately see that I wasn't some crazed fan but an average angst-ridden dude just like him minus the deep-seated daddy issues and heroin addiction. I wouldn't ask him about music because everyone did that. Instead, I was going to ask him about his house and how he found it. Nothing says "average normal guy" like someone talking to you about your house.

By the end of the first conversation we'd be laughing and he'd say something like, "Why don't you come up and check out the house?" and then I'd say (and here is the genius part of it), "I can't do it today but maybe later this week." What? Could I be any less of a fan when I turned down an invite to the casa? In my mind, and believe me I played it out several times, it was foolproof. Of course, it never happened and the one time I did see him by Lake Washington, it was about ninety degrees and he was huddled up on a park bench wearing a hooded sweatshirt and a wool coat. I guess it's a good thing that I was minus the daddy issues and heroin.

You know who else I did that with in my head when I first got to Los Angeles? Tori Spelling. In my mind I thought, "She's successful but for sure not out of my league." And it didn't take me long to figure out what our first conversation was going to be. I would pretend I didn't know who she was. You know, the ole "I'm Josh. What's your name?" ruse. Because that would show her that I didn't care who she was, which would immediately disarm her. She'd think, "This guy actually wants to get to know me for me, not because I'm Tori Spelling." The fly was heading right for the web.

I'd ask her what she did and when she told me I'd say

(and I like to refer to this line as "the panty dropper"), "Sorry, I don't really watch TV." *Bam!* From there it was going to be gravy. I figured Tori Spelling was going to be my entry into the lap of luxury, parties at the Viper Room, meetings with her dad who would create a show around me, an appearance on *Letterman* with me telling him the story about how Tori and I met, and then ultimately my ending things with her after my first feature-film love scene and eventual torrid affair with Salma Hayek.

I had the whole thing mapped out and I actually did bump into her at the movies once just the way I had always thought it would happen. You know what I said? Nothing. I might have mumbled something about how I "love *90210*" and I think she might have said something like, "That's nice."

Realizing that I wasn't going to be able to make a living off a chance meeting with someone famous, I walked around downtown Seattle, Pioneer Square to be specific, looking for work as a bartender. Luckily, this was way before bar owners got smart and started hiring hot chicks to bartend.

Guys are so stupid. It has always made me laugh when I see a guy give a good-looking bartender a big tip. It's so obvious why he's doing it. He thinks there's a shot that he'll get laid. That's the reason we do ninety-five percent of everything we do! Just for the shot, just on the off chance that it *might* lead to us getting laid.

It's like when we're in traffic and we wave a good-looking woman in front of us so she can cut in. What do we think is going to happen? That she's going to pay us back by blowing us on the side of the road? None of us believe that it's actually going to happen, but we're willing to take the chance. Like my father always said, "You've got to play the lottery to win it."

That job-hunt day in Seattle I got rejection after rejection. At my last stop, two things struck me right away: how different it looked from the rest of the places on the Square and how much emptier it was. Those two things stayed true during my entire stay in the city.

I asked a Japanese woman if I could talk to the manager about a job, and she told me that she was the manager. This woman later became one of my best friends. It turned out that she wasn't Japanese. Or even Asian for that matter. Not sure how I made that mistake exactly. Maybe because I had been in the middle of my Asian-woman fetish and I was hoping that every woman I met was Asian. Or maybe, after being in Seattle for about a week and seeing more Asian women than I had in my entire life, I was seeing Asian. (FYI, I just coined that phrase, my friends: Seeing Asian. Might make some T-shirts.)

My first day at work there I realized two really bad

things: It cost seven bucks a day to park and (gulp) there were no hats allowed inside. What? The place where there was a Styrofoam "castle" wall separating the kitchen from the dining area was too classy for hats? Did I mention that I had hair down to my ass at this point?

Now may be the time to try to explain my love affair with hats. Where do I start?

Let's start with the fact that I love baseball. A couple of years ago I had the opportunity to go down on the field and take batting practice with the Mariners, and I had to pull my sweatshirt down over my boner. I heard Ken Griffey Jr. say, "Why is that dude staring at me?" I stole a bag of sunflower seeds. Big time baseball nerd.

Needless to say, when I was growing up, I wore a lot of baseball hats. And for some reason, I really started to dig the way the hats gave a little extra curl to my Jew fro. For those of you who aren't Jewish or don't believe a Jew fro is an actual thing, do a Google image search and then get back to me.

I grew up with three older brothers, which means I got my ass kicked a lot and was subjected to some serious mental torture. For years, my brothers called me Squash. Not sure exactly why that bothered me so much but it did. And my brother Danny figured out that nothing was a more sure-fire way to get me to cry than to play Barry Manilow's "Weekend in New England."

You heard me.

Danny played that song over and over and over. I'm not sure if my crying started as a joke or a way to get attention or just so I could get a break from getting my ass beat. Hell, maybe the song really made me cry. All I know is that after he saw that first tear fall, he played "Weekend" *a lot.*

The mental torture didn't stop with Barry Manilow. You know that stage in your life when you seriously look like a science experiment gone bad? You get out of the shower and you still smell and you're still greasy and the zits you popped have already grown back bigger and stronger. For guys, there are so many hormones rushing through your body that just putting on underwear gives you a hard-on. Anything brushing up against your Johnson puts you in danger of embarrassing yourself in front of your entire eighth-grade math class.

You can always tell a guy with a chubby when he's walking down the hallway. Guys carry their books to the side. That's just how we do it. Dudes without hard-ons, that is. Dudes with chubbies carry their books right up front with two hands. All the other guys know what's going on, and there's always that one asshole who will come along, knock the books out of your hands, and point at your aggressive little friend, who is standing at attention.

Those are tough years on everyone. You are so self-conscious about every little thing about your own body, and the slightest mention about anything having to do with your physical appearance can send you into a yearlong tailspin. Well, at some point, one of my brothers decided that I had a big forehead. I believe he started calling it an "eighthead" because it was twice as big as a normal one. At first I didn't think twice about it because I figured he was just being an asshole but then I made the mistake of asking my mom and you know what she said?

"That's ridiculous, honey. It just means you're extra smart."

Uh-oh. Extra smart? Meaning more brains? Meaning you need more room for more brains...meaning humongous forehead. Fuuuuuuuuuuuck!

After that, anytime I saw my reflection, I'd think, "You need a SWAT team to rappel down that slope!"

Knowing that it finally got to me, my brothers stepped on the gas. "Hey, Josh, NASA called and they were wondering why there was a planet in our house." Or, "Hey, Squash, I wanna practice my forehand, bring your head over here!" And on and on it went. Needless to say, a bit of a complex arose and I wore a hat every single day after that.

Now, you would think that as soon as I got a little older and wiser and more self-confident, I would have laughed at how sensitive I was about those insults and lost the hat.

Uh … who in the world has that much confidence?

Once you think that about yourself you are done. Why do you think plastic surgeons make so much money? Someone, at some time, told a girl that her C cup would look much better as a G and ta-da, more insecurities were born. So I wore a hat in junior high and I wore a hat for most of high school and I wore a hat in college and, yup, you guessed it, I wore a hat when I got to Seattle.

No, I don't sleep with the hat on. No, I don't shower with the hat on. Yes, I have had sex with the hat on but it's not a prerequisite. Although some girls have in the past requested that I leave the hat on. Not because they didn't like me without it but because it was how they had always pictured sex with me. Who am I to question why?

There were times when I took the hat off, like my first few appearances on Chelsea's show, but a lot of weird things came up. First, you can only imagine how pale one half of my forehead is, and since I'm already insecure about the length of my forehead, highlighting half of it sends me into a bit of a tizzy.

Second, people did not recognize me when I took my hat off, which ended up being bad for my comedy *and* my confidence. I had worn a hat for a long time and developed a certain personality that went along with it. When I took it off, I became very self-conscious of people talking about me not having a hat. All I could think about was why everyone was staring at my head, which didn't exactly lend itself to funny.

My hat turned into a vicious little trap. Even now, I'd love to take it off but I've painted myself into such a corner.

Now back to Seattle…

I was bartending, hat off, one Friday night at the upstairs bar and it was the same old shit. For some reason, the owner thought it was a good idea to put out a $2.99 all-you-can-eat appetizer buffet from 8 to 10 PM because it would help bring a crowd. It brought in a crowd all right but not the crowd you wanted. It brought in a crowd that you would expect to see at a fucking $2.99 appetizer buffet.

Since we were right next to a homeless shelter, our place was packed with homeless folks who loaded up on food for two hours straight. It was like that scene from *Trading Places* when Dan Aykroyd starts stuffing food into his Santa suit.

Around 10 PM, as the homeless started to clear out, our DJ started to spin. Worst DJ of all time, by the way. A short, skinny black guy named Dante who had the *greasiest* curls I have ever seen. He had this fifty-year-old white girlfriend who he had convinced that he was going to be the most famous DJ in the world.

All night she would come up to the bar to get his Hennessey in a snifter, with four ice cubes, grenadine, and a splash of Coke. "You know Dante can't spin unless you add that splash of Coke." She told me every night that he would pay for the drinks when he hit it big.

I knew that he was never going to pay for the drinks but the reason I gave them to him was because the drunker he got, the more horrible he was and to me that made the night much funnier. After about three drinks, he would start talking on the mic between songs. "This is Dante up in this mothafucka! Ha-ha! If this next song don't shake yo' ass, then Dante's gonna come out there and shake it for ya! Let's see some cheeks!" It was hilarious.

"Let's see some cheeks" is still one of my favorite things I have ever heard.

That Friday night, as Dante started, or as he would put it, "It's time for Dante to make this mothafucka do the choo-choo" (I wish I was making that up), two white girls sat down at the end of the bar.

Since the dance floor was downstairs, my bar was dead, and since my bar was dead, that meant I spent the entire night feeding these two girls Malibu Bay Breezes. When I first started bartending, a buddy of mine who slung drinks down the street told me that if the goal is vagina, keep pouring the Malibu Bay Breeze.

The goal is always vagina.

Plus, hatless, I wasn't (and still am not) a very confident guy, so I figured I needed to get them as drunk as I could.

I basically stood in front of the two girls cracking jokes, pouring obscenely strong drinks, and thinking that I might actually close the deal. I know, I know. A bartender takes home a drunk chick, what's the big deal? It was a big deal for me because I hadn't kissed, much less had sex, with anyone since The Girl who had crushed and flushed me. I must have gone about six months with zero Vinny-Jay. It was time to break the streak.

Don't get me wrong, I had some opportunities at the club. There was this one girl who asked me to have sex with her almost every Friday night. She was a black girl who had *huuuuuuuuge* boobs and an enormous ass. Jimmy used to tell me, "Your dick has got to be at least ten inches long just to make it past those cheeks!" Huge boobs and big butt is basically my thing, but I still couldn't do it with her.

And it wasn't because she was black. By that point in my life, I had already slept with my fair share of black girls. As a matter of fact, a good chunk of my high school career was spent deeply entrenched in the hip-hop culture. My first concert ever was Run-DMC, I was a member of the break dancing group The Jamherst Breakers (J-Rock was my name, bitches), and I know it sounds as cliché as it can get, but my best friend in high school was black.

The problem wasn't the color of her skin. It was that I was pretty sure she could kick my ass. She was like Serena Williams's trainer. Huge. Part of me thought, "Why not? Let's give this shit a try for sure." This wasn't like the body builder single mom I encountered later in Los Angeles. When this woman talked about having sex with me, she made it sound like there was going to be a lot of pain in my future. She was the first and only woman whose physical presence and attitude intimidated me out of sleeping with her. Don't get me wrong, I have definitely tried some stuff just to see what it was like. For example, one of the black women I did sleep with was huge. But not Serena huge. She was more Nell Carter huge. Way less threatening.

I had always talked to a few of my friends about the crazy curiosity I had with having sex with a really big woman. I just wanted to know how it was different. Or was it? Shit, I had no idea, and since none of my friends shared the same thirst for knowledge, it was up to me to find out.

I was living in upstate New York with my parents after I graduated from college. I needed to save up some cash before I moved to Seattle and living rent free with home cooking was the best way to do that. I had also found a job bartending at a place that was right on the New York–Connecticut border. Those bars were generally pretty dead until the bars in Connecticut closed and then thousands of drunk people would get in their cars and head for New York for some more drinks.

One night I was bartending and it was packed at about 2 AM. As I was making a round of Slippery Nipples, I saw this enormous black woman sitting at the end of the bar all alone. This was not a bar that generally had a lot of black folks in it. As a matter of fact, it was usually packed with hicks who sounded like Tony Soprano. Never got used to that.

She sat there by herself for the whole night, just stirring her drink, and as things were winding down, I walked over to talk to her. It turns out she had been stood up. She was supposed to meet a blind date and he just never showed. I didn't have the heart to tell her that what probably happened was that he walked in, saw her, and said, "Fuck that." He then went straight back to his house, called whoever set him up, and asked them what the hell they were thinking.

She had me laughing as I was cleaning up and when it was time for everyone to clear out, she asked me if I wanted to get something to eat after my shift. At this point, I still wasn't thinking anything naughty. All I knew was that she was funny and I was hungry. I could either eat alone or with her.

At the diner she had me rolling! She actually threatened

to eat the waitress if she didn't get the food to our table in under ten minutes. When the food came, she kept firing jokes until there was a brief pause in the conversation and then she asked, "You ever been with a black woman?"

Have you ever been in a situation that you thought was one thing and when it turns out to be something else you got uncomfortable? I thought I was sitting at a booth, sharing a meal with a new funny friend, but then all of a sudden I was thinking, "Am I on a date?" Things changed that quickly.

"Been...?" I asked.

"Fucked," she said, erasing any chance that I was misinterpreting what she was asking.

The answer was yes but that wasn't what was going through my head. For the first time that night it dawned on me that I might actually be able to cross something off my list.

The list, by the way, is something that most men have in their head. Or on paper if they're rookies. The last thing you want is for anyone to find your list. It includes things you want to do or see. This is not the "Go to Paris" or "Swim with the dolphins" list. This list is "Bang someone in the circus" or "Poop in a mailbox." Things you want to do but you don't want other people to know you want to do.

And wouldn't you know it but "Sex with Nell Carter" was on my list.

It didn't take too long for me to decide what I was going to do. I was going to finish my meal and have sex with this woman. Not a doubt in my mind. After all, how many things do you really ever get to cross off that list?

I was in.

Without giving you the details, let me just say it was different for sure. Not better, not worse, just different. There's just a whole lot more going on when you have sex with someone that big. A lot more variables that you need to worry about. Also, at that time I weighed only about a hundred and sixty pounds soaking wet with rocks in my pockets, so I really had to be careful about what position I found myself in.

It was the only time in my life that I had to say, "I can't breathe!" during sex. The no air—not really my thing. Not sure what David Carradine saw in it exactly, but different strokes for different folks. Pun intended.

So back to Seattle. After six long months with no magic whoo-whoo, it looked like that night might be the night. The Malibu Bay Breezes were working like a charm, Dante was spinning the worst music of all time so the girls never left my bar, I was throwing out all the tricks I knew to keep them entertained and apparently my giant forehead hadn't ruined the mood.

The next challenge was to try to separate the two of them. I was interested in the dark-haired woman, and as

I was trying to concoct the perfect, witty one-liner that would make her leave her friend, she walked right up to me and said, "I bet you look good naked." It was that easy. Not for me...for her!

Can you imagine if a guy tried that line on a girl? He'd get punched in the nuts by her and her friends...repeatedly! "I bet you look good naked?" You could try that a million times and it would never work on a girl. Not once. You could try it a million times on a guy and it would work every fucking time.

We are pigs.

And stupid.

Vaginas rule the school.

That woman...did not have sex with me that night. That woman...I dated for the rest of my time in Seattle. That woman...already had two kids (ages two and six months). That woman...gave birth to my youngest son. That woman...moved to California with me.

We split up about eighteen months after we moved to Los Angeles. She ended up leaving Los Angeles and going back to Seattle but I kept all the kids for a little while so she could get herself settled in and stable.

So when my new wife started talking about kids, I thought, "What? I've been doing this, and a lot of it solo, since I was twenty-five! Don't get me wrong, I love my kids and would do anything in the world for them but...I can see the finish line!" I started telling her about all the things that we would be able to do in a few years. The trips we would be able to take, the way we would be able to really pursue our careers at full speed, and that for once in our relationship it would be just us.

When Beth joined this nuthouse, we made an instant family. She loved and looked after the kids like they were her own but we truly never had a chance to just be a couple. Our "courting period" involved Chuck E. Cheese. Not sure how fair that was to her but she stuck it out. Reason number 172 why she's the best. (Not just saying that for pity sex, but I think there's a good chance I'll get it after she reads this paragraph.)

When we started dating she always said she wanted kids but she never pushed it because our lives, between getting to know each other, work, and kids, were so crazy. And honestly, selfishly, I thought that maybe she would see that we were already enough. Years passed, and a baby never happened. Beth had stopped talking about babies as much so I thought she had decided it wasn't going to happen.

Nope.

One day, I was in the bedroom and I heard my youngest son start to cry and call for me. I ran outside and found Beth sitting next to him in the front yard. His foot was bleeding a little bit. I sat down next to them and Beth said, "He cut his foot on something."

"You okay, buddy?" I asked my son.

"It just really stings," he said, as Beth got up and went inside.

I carried him in and fixed the foot, blah, blah, blah. After I got my son all set in his room, I went looking for Beth. She was in the bedroom making the bed. Uh-oh. Something was wrong. She would never go into the bedroom in the middle of the day and start making the bed if nothing was wrong. We're not neat freaks and we're not messy either, but we're definitely not the people who decide to make the bed in the middle of the day if we forget to do it in the morning.

"Everything okay?" I asked. I knew the answer but also knew that she would say nothing was wrong and that meant something was wrong and that I should stay in the room and talk to her until she told me what was wrong.

See? I was learning something!

"I'm fine," she said.

I was right! I couldn't believe she actually said what I thought she would say! Fuck, part of me wanted to come out and tell her how proud I was of myself, that after countless relationships and arguments I had finally figured out how to play this game. However, I wisely resisted the urge to act like a dumbass and I plodded on.

"Are you sure? It just seems like something's bothering you."

73

"It's nothing."

She was already starting to crack? After only one recheck? Holy shit, something was really bothering her.

"Beth, what's wrong?"

She tucked the sheets in *really hard* and said, "He called for you."

"Huh?"

"When he cut his foot he called for you."

"I don't get it. You're upset because he called for me to help him?"

"No, I think the fact that he calls for you when he's hurt is beautiful. The fact that you're the person he thinks of, that you're the person he thinks can save him is amazing and your relationship with your kids is one of the things I love the most about you."

She snapped the pillows into the pillowcases and took a deep breath. "I just want someone to love me the way they love you," she said, holding back tears.

Are you kidding me? Have I really been the most selfish prick in the entire world and this woman still stayed with me? If I could have pushed out an ass-baby right there I would have.

I had told my story so many times about taking care of the kids by myself and getting an instant family at a young age that I had completely forgotten (or blindly chosen to ignore) that she had done the same thing. She had come in, set her own ego aside, and stepped up to the plate just like I did.

Since I had the kids by myself, I wasn't playing second fiddle to anyone. I never felt like an outsider or the babysitter. She did. Not anyone's fault, it just was the way it was. I had to fix that. So you know what that meant it was time for?

Lots of sex with no condoms.

I wish raising them was as fun as making them.

P.S. I hate blood. Can't stand it. But having a kid gives you tolerance for things. Things you never thought you'd be able to take and somehow you do. Before I had kids, watching people throw up—hell, just hearing them throw up—would send me running to the bathroom. Not anymore. My son has shit on my finger. He has peed in my mouth. In my *mouth*!

It wasn't like he was nine and stood over my bed and peed in my mouth. I definitely would have had a problem with that. It happened when I was changing his diaper. Same thing with the poop on the finger.

Thought it couldn't hurt to explain that one too.

CHAPTER 4

Kids Are Pussies

Kids are pussies.

Let me be more specific. This generation of kids are pussies. They're a bunch of soft, entitled, heads-in-their-cell-phones, never-mowed-a-lawn-a-day-in-their-lives, candy-ass pussies. Yeah, I said it. I said what you all are thinking but are scared to say, because nobody wants to hurt their fragile little psyches.

Ugh. At some point in time, someone, somewhere in this country decided that nothing bad should happen to kids ever. We decided that we had to protect them from *everything* that could possibly upset them in any way, and that is fucked up. Some kids spend their whole childhood growing up without hearing the word no.

Are you kidding me? My dad used to say no as we were walking up to him. He had a T-shirt that said no so he wouldn't even have to talk to us. He could just point at his T-shirt. My dad named my first dog No. I used to think it was kind of an asshole move but I don't think so anymore.

It's not that I want to say no to everything, and I'm sure he didn't either, it's just that no is easier. If you say yes, there's a possibility there might be more planning and different levels to the conversation. There are some things that I've wanted to say yes to but I knew if I did, it would mean me getting up off my ass and driving somewhere. Or, even worse, having one of my kids' annoying friends at the house.

Speaking of which, that's the worst—when your kid has a friend who just annoys the shit out of you. Oh. My. God. I know my kids aren't perfect and I'm sure they are the annoying friends at some people's houses but, wowsers, some of the kids who have been at my house...I can't even describe.

There was one kid—and I don't want to say his name because he actually turned into a really good kid, so let's call him Evan—who was the single most annoying person I have ever met in my life. He would sit at the dinner table and, at ten years old, say things like, "This is not good. Do you guys eat this kind of food all the time?"

There was one night when he told me that he couldn't watch TV at our house anymore because he didn't like the smell of my couch. He actually told me once that he really

Josh Wolf

liked coming to our house because "I can put anything anywhere and I don't really feel like I have to clean it up."

I hated Evan. I know, I know, I can hear some of you already: "How could you hate him? He was just a kid." Yup. A kid I hated.

His mother told me once, "The thing I like the most about Evan is that he's not afraid to speak his mind. Don't you think that's great?" No, because that's the exact thing that makes me hate him. He was the type of kid who felt he could say anything to anyone, including his parents, because they didn't want to "stifle him." Stifle him? I wanted to smother him. I heard him tell his mother to fuck off. Seriously. He screamed at her in front of the school, "Oh why don't you just fuck off!" I was ready to hold him down so she could go straight gangsta on his ass, but do you know what she did? Nothing. Instead, she said, "Oh, Evan. I know you can choose better words to express how you feel."

Not really. "Fuck off" pretty much expresses "fuck off" as well as anyone can express it. If that was the only problem she had with him saying it, then she was wrong.

The *real* problem was that she let him say it and the police didn't come and question her about child abuse later that day. If any of my kids ever told me to fuck off, they better get ready to either run or fight because something is going down for sure.

I know some of you are wondering why the hell I let this little asshole into my house. Valid question and there are a few answers. To be clear, he didn't swear at me, and the one time he did swear in my house I made it pretty clear that it wasn't going to fly under my roof.

He said, "This fucking sucks" when we couldn't make it to a movie.

I told him that nobody talked like that in my house.

He responded, "Well, I don't live here."

To which I responded, with my face right in his and my hands firmly on his shoulder, "Go ahead and swear again and see how it goes for you."

He never swore again.

But as much of a dickhead as he was, he was really funny. I mean fucking hilarious. Some of the incredibly rude things he said were so outrageous, they killed me. The kid just flat out had great timing and a fantastic wit, and in my world, funny goes a long way. Another reason I let him in the house was because he and my youngest son got along really well. No arguments, no drama, just silence.

I can't explain to you how important that is. The best part about having somebody else's kid at your house is that you don't have to do anything. They entertain each other. I always pushed my kids to have people over and it made them think I was the coolest guy ever because they constantly had friends hanging around. Cool? Are you kidding? I had them over so I wouldn't have to talk to them. I mean, it was cool all right, but not for the reasons they're saying it was.

We finally had to cut ties with Evan though, because one night he said something that went way over the line. Jacob, Evan, and I were in the living room watching the Red Sox when my wife, Beth, walked into the room. She didn't say anything; she didn't even look in our direction, as a matter of fact. I'm pretty sure she was just grabbing something and walking out, but Evan felt he had something to say...and he did. He said, "Did those jeans used to fit you?"

Uh...what?

My wife is a good-looking woman with a pretty killer body and I'm not just saying that because I would get killed if I didn't. She is pretty fuckin' hot. But asking someone if their jeans used to fit is basically saying, "Those jeans can no longer contain you" or "How the fuck did you squeeze your fat ass into those?"

Beth didn't even acknowledge that Evan had said anything. She just grabbed the car keys and on her way out of the room said, "Josh, can I talk to you for a second?" That was the last we saw of Evan.

I guarantee the reason Evan felt like he could say anything to anyone and do what he wanted was because his parents never said no to him. You have to. Saying no also ends conversations, or it should anyway.

I know there are plenty of people who let their kids ask "why" a million times. I learned that was just a slow way to drive yourself crazy. I heard a woman on the playground once tell her son to stop spitting at the other kids and the kid said, "Why?"

"Because you might hurt their feelings or give them a headache," she said.

"Why?" he asked again.

He asked "why" about three more times. Uh, no sir. If that had happened in my house?

Me: Don't spit at people.

Kid: Why?

Me: Because I'll kill the Easter Bunny, that's why. Don't spit.

End of story.

Kids are coddled and pampered. Did you know that there are a lot of schools in this great country of ours that have outlawed dodgeball? Dodgeball! They say that it humiliates the kids. Which, ironically, is why we played the fucking game to begin with. It was a great lesson in life! At a very early age you learned about pecking order and hierarchy. You learned about alliances and self-preservation. You learned that people who you think are friends will sell you out just so they don't get hurt or embarrassed. Lastly, you learned that red rubber does not taste good at all. Even to this day I remember what it tastes like on my lips. *Bam!* The ball hits you, your eyes water, your nose runs, and you try to walk off the court but— *Bam! Bam! Bam!*—nine other balls hit you and then you scream, "I'm out already! Shit! Fuck! I am out!"

I have to admit, I was pretty good at dodgeball. I actually had a move that made me damn near unhittable. Looking back, I'm pretty sure we all had the same move but at the time I thought mine was the best. It's that move when you jump up and throw your legs out so it looks like you're doing the splits in the air. I called it the—are you ready for this piece of shit name?—I called it the Outer Space Legger. You heard me. And worse than the name? I used to fucking scream it after I did it. I would jump, the ball would fly through my legs, and when I landed I would scream, "Outer Space Legger!" Don't ask me why. The better question is why didn't someone punch me in the face and stop me from saying that ever again?

Also, I used to stretch out before dodgeball. Just writing that makes me feel like an asshole, but you know what was worse? While I was stretching I would turn to my friends and say, "Hope you guys don't have to see too many OSLs this recess or it's gonna get ugly." OSL = Outer Space Legger. I was the typical semiathletic jerkoff who, up until the age of fifteen, pretended gym class was the fucking Olympics.

I remember when my son's school told the kids they couldn't play dodgeball because they were getting "too competitive." That's the same group of fucktards who think that every kid who plays Little League should get a trophy. You should not get a trophy for sucking!

Whiny, stereotypical parent voice: "But the children should learn that what's important is how you play the game and that we are all winners."

No, we're not! We are not all winners. Think about the people you work with. How many of them would you actually classify as winners? You think they deserve a trophy for coming to work and doing a shitty job? Hell, I'd rather give a trophy to the guy who walks around crop-dusting his office all day. (Crop-dusting is the art of farting silently while walking.) At least that takes some kind of skill.

Kids need to learn at some point in their lives that not everything is possible and we're not all winners. You can't squash their dreams but you have to be realistic with them, for shit's sake. My son was talking about how he wanted to play in the NBA and he asked me what I thought about it. What was I supposed to do? Lie?

I told him, "Listen, you can try to do whatever you want but the truth is that you are a skinny Jew. I'm 5′10″ on a good day and your mom wasn't a hair over 5′6″. Now, you could own an NBA team. That might be something you can look into, but as far as playing on one? I might turn to golf or tennis if I were you."

Nobody tells kids the truth and that's why they all think they deserve a trophy. "I tried my hardest. Where's my trophy?" It doesn't work like that. Shit, I wish it did. I wish it worked like that with everything:

"I tried my hardest. Can we still have sex?"

"I tried my hardest. Can I still get the job?"

"I tried my hardest. Can the defendant go free?"

As much as I can't stand the attitude of the kids, it's the parents who are to blame for sure. It's ridiculous. It's that whole "All kids are good. All children are beautiful" bullshit. All kids are beautiful is the biggest load of crap ever. Really? All kids are good-looking? What about the ones you see at the park with the heads that are too big and the eyes that are real far apart? They look like ET fucked a dolphin.

Everyone can't be perfect and the sooner you learn that in life, the better off I think you'll be. Kids get an inflated view of themselves...because of their parents. They have a sense of entitlement....because of their parents. They treat other people like servants...because of their parents. "But we're just trying to raise a positive person who can contribute to society." That sounds like a good idea; why don't you do that. Because right now you're raising little assholes who can't solve problems and who expect people to do everything for them.

This generation is taught in school that if someone says something to you that you don't like, go tell a teacher. If I went to the guy who used to oversee our recess and told him that someone called me an asshole, he would have said, "Well, you probably deserved it." And you know what? I probably did. They made us solve our own problems.

I got called into my son's school one day because he had been in a fight on the playground. I sat next to him across from the principal, who said, "Mr. Wolf, I want to thank you for coming in so quickly. I truly believe it's important that our kids see the school and parents working together on the same team."

Okay.

She went on. "It seems that Jacob punched another boy at recess today and when I asked him about it he said that you told him to do it. I assured him that he must have been mistaken and I told him that I would call you in right away so you could explain yourself a little better." She nodded for me to explain.

"Is this the kid who's been picking on you?" I asked my son.

"Yes."

"Did you warn him that if he kept picking on you, you would punch him in the face?"

"Mmm-hmm," he said.

"Did he keep picking on you?"

"Yes."

"And then?

"And then I punched him in the face."

I turned back to the principal and said, "No, he got it right. That's exactly what I told him."

She nearly lost her fucking mind.

"Use your words. Use your words." That's what these people are constantly telling the kids. Use your words? Pretty soon the only words these kids will be saying are "Ouch! Give me my lunch money back" and "Why did you steal my girlfriend?"

I know some of you have already started blogging about how stupid and irresponsible I am and blah-fuckin'-blah. I'm not saying that kids should fight all of the time. You should in fact always do your best to avoid a physical confrontation, but the truth is sometimes you just can't. I always told Jacob that sometimes the only thing a bully understands is a punch in the mouth.

I will admit that you do kinda have to be careful with your message though. It's hard to make a ten-year-old see the line between when he can punch and when he can't. And I have to admit that I eventually had to reel Jacob in a bit.

Well, "a bit" may be understating it some.

The next few weeks he was punching people left and right. You cut in front of me? You're a bully! *Bam!* You think my shoes are ugly? You're a bully! *Bam!* You're sitting in my seat at lunch? Uh...you're not a bully but I'm gonna punch you anyway! *Bam!*

I had to sit him down and explain to him that it was okay to hit someone if you were defending yourself or someone you love. You never start a fight but it is okay to finish one. I thought he got it. I mean he said he got it. Turns out, he didn't really get it.

We were at my friend's house for a BBQ with a bunch of other families one Sunday. There was a full-court basketball game out front that the fathers were playing in (nothing too spectacular, all white guys over thirty), one of those moon-bounce things (or as I like to call them, grope houses) in the back, and a huge BBQ pit on the side of the house. All in all, there were well over a hundred people there.

It was one of those Hollywood parties that was disguised as a family get-together but everyone was in the business and talking about the business from the moment they arrived. On top of that, the guy who owned the house was pretty big in TV land and it was always a good idea to stop by his place to see who would be there. Jacob liked going with me because the house was amazing and he got along well with my friend's oldest son.

There were always a lot of teenagers at these parties, which I liked and didn't like at the same time. I liked it because I always thought it was good for Jacob to hang around older kids. Nothing wrong with not being the biggest or fastest and getting teased a little to keep you in line. I didn't like it because all teenagers are fuckin' know-it-alls.

Jacob would come home saying, "I know. I know. I know" because that's what they say to everything. "I know." No, you don't know. You don't know shit actually. Did you know that? If you knew anything, you wouldn't be tucking those skinny jeans into those high-tops like that because you look ridiculous. Did you know that? And take the sticker off your hat! Did you already buy the hat? Then take the fucking sticker off it!

And they would just walk around all day taking pictures... of themselves. What? "Look, this is a picture of me." Snap! "This is a picture of my shoes." Snap! "This is a picture of me in the mirror taking a picture of myself taking a picture of myself!" Snap! I've got an idea, why don't you take a picture of yourself next to a fucking job application? How about that?

Can you imagine if this generation had to do something important? What if these kids were the ones who had to storm the beaches of Normandy? Are you picturing these kids out there on those boats? Flippin' their Justin Bieber bangs out of their eyes, everybody named Trevor, Travis, or Tyler, not knowing how to get to the beach because nobody has the beach app on their phone, and all of them probably getting shot because they posed for a picture in front of the boat to post on Facebook!

So at that BBQ party I was playing in this full-court game and, if I do say so myself, I was doing pretty well. Look, nobody is ever going to confuse me for a good basketball player—to be honest with you, I got cut from the freshman basketball team. Do you know how bad I had to be to get cut from *my* freshman basketball team? We lost to the deaf school. We were bad. (Side note: The deaf kids played extremely hard. Talk about playing until the whistle. Wow. I'm imagining that one team at one time pretended that the whistle blew, tricked them, and they made sure they would never fall for that again.)

By the way, I've stopped playing pick-up basketball. I can no longer stand to rub up against those sweaty fuckers. The older guys get, the hairier and sweatier they become, and sometimes you get that disgustingly sweaty T-shirt just swooshing right down your face. Yuck. I've almost puked on the court because some guy turned quickly and the sweat from his face went into my mouth. I seriously thought that I was going to lose it right there. I ran off the court, to the parking lot, into my car, to my house for a shower, and then gargled with tequila. It's the number one reason I could never do that mixed martial arts stuff. As soon as someone's sweaty ass crack was in my face I would tap out. Well, besides the fact that I'm a pussy.

So I was dominating this basketball game and as I looked down to the other end of the court, I saw Jacob punching my friend's kid right in the face. No! Don't punch his kid! Not only did his house provide us with food every Sunday and not only could almost every person at this party offer me a job, but hadn't you seen the way I was schooling these old clowns?

We ran down to the other end of the court and I grabbed Jacob by the arm. Any parent will tell you that if you're in a group and your kid is the one who gets in trouble, you feel like a fucking leper. You can sense other people staring at you, judging you. It's the same feeling you get when you have a small child who has a big bruise and you're in line at the supermarket. You feel like everyone is looking at you and wondering how your kid got that big-ass bruise. You find yourself saying things out loud like, "I can't believe you ran into the tree like that, can you, buddy? Crazy how it gave you that big bruise on your arm right there." That sentence is code for "I don't beat my kid." Not sure "code" is actually the right word because it implies that sentence might be tough to crack and it certainly isn't.

You get that same kind of feeling when your kid acts out in public, but there are two very different kinds of responses.

The first type of response is to just apologize to everyone and everything who is within earshot. "I am so sorry about this. I don't know what got into him. He usually plays so well with other kids. There's no excuse for this and you can be sure that he will be punished. I promise you that." That shit usually goes on for as long as it takes for the parent to backpedal out of there, bowing like a Japanese man at a business meeting.

The second response is the parent just starts defending their kid for no good reason. This is the type of parent who, even if they saw a videotape of their kid kicking someone out of an airplane and screaming, "I hate Jews," would say, "He didn't mean it. My Tony is a nice, nice boy." This group of annoying people brags incessantly about their kids and fills your inbox with baby pictures.

That's the worst, isn't it? "Look, here's baby Norma in her crib. And here she is outside and here she is lying down." Enough! Norma is an infant, which means two things. One, *all* babies look the same. All of them! And two, the only expression infants have on their face is the "I have gas" face. That's it. That's their range. I don't need to see another picture that looks like every other picture of every other fucking baby. Mine included.

And then they start to brag.

Ironically, it's the people who shouldn't be bragging about their kids who do. "Little Joey is such a good reader. He just breezes through everything we give him and he loves it. I can't believe what an amazing reader he is. It's truly unbelievable." Shut up. First of all, he's twelve. He should be reading, and second, I don't give a flying fuck. Let me make a rule that I think everyone would be happy to have in place: If we don't share the same last name, stop telling me, showing me, or explaining to me anything about your kid! If I don't ask, I don't care.

So, when I run into one of these situations, I don't actually know which reaction I'm going to use until I feel out the crowd. If it's a good group of people who are polite and let me do the parenting, I'm the first type of person. If it's a group of people who start lashing out and say things to my kid, I'm the second type.

Parenting Rule #1: I always teach my kids that, no matter what, we stick together.

That means I would stick up for him in that crowd. I would have his back all the way until we got in our car and started to drive away and then I would rip into him. You never want them to think you're choosing other people over them because someday those little monsters who are running around your house, stealing the change out of your top drawer, and cheating on their homework might have to wipe your ass when you can't. Just something to keep in the back of your head.

When I ran over, the group was very cool. Nobody was yelling at me or Jacob so I chose reaction number one. I apologized repeatedly, checked on my buddy's son, apologized again, and had Jacob apologize. I basically kissed everyone's ass who was within a hundred feet of the court, said good-bye to anyone who would listen, and took off.

When we got in the car I started to tear my son a new asshole. "I can't believe you did that! What did I tell you about punching people? You only do it if you're defending yourself or somebody you love. Nobody wants to hang around with someone who is punching them all of the time, Jacob." I laid into him for a good fifteen minutes and the entire time he just stared at me. He didn't cry, he didn't look upset...he just stared. Finally, I said, "Are you going to say anything at all?"

He said, "I did exactly what you said, Dad."

"You did? He was threatening you?"

"No."

"He was threatening someone you love?"

"Well, no, but..."

"But what?" I asked.

"You said that it was okay to hit someone if you were defending someone you love."

"That's right, I did."

"That's what I did," he said.

"Really?" I said, not believing a word he was saying. "And who were you defending?"

"You."

"Me?"

"Yeah. We were watching you guys play and Daulton said that his dad was a better basketball player than you and I said he wasn't even close. He said it a couple more times and then he said that at least his dad didn't drive a minivan so I punched him."

Holy shit, he was listening. He was defending me. His action was still clearly over the line and he didn't need to punch someone in the face. But he didn't like the way someone was talking about his dad so he laid him out. It's this kind of moment that leaves you with some faith that you're actually doing some good.

I'm sure every generation looks at the generation after them and thinks the same exact thing. When I was rockin' a mullet and wearing jeans way past my waist and a tank top, my father must have looked at me and thought, "This is the stupidest generation ever." He must have been baffled by my Walkman and why kids "always have to have your music with you. Can't you just have some peace and quiet in your head?"

We all complain about the youth because we don't

understand them, I guess. But then something happens. Something that shows you a glimpse of their humanity, that gives you a reminder that they know they're not the only ones on this earth. And it makes them a little more tolerable.

CHAPTER 5

Don't Be a Douchebag

W hy do people turn into such douchebags immediately after they have kids?

It's like they forget who they are and how to have fun as soon as that little bastard peeks his head out of the honey hole. I'm not saying you should keep up the same lifestyle you had before you got a kid. I think Child Protective Services calls that "neglect." You can, however, continue to live your life. The worst is the person who can't have a conversation with you without bringing up their kid. It's like they don't have an opinion anymore. They only eat, think, shit, and breathe their kid.

There's a guy I know who, no matter what you're talking about, swings it back to his son. I always take the conversation as far away from his kid as I can just to see how he's going to get back to him. I might say something like, "Can you believe what's going on in Iran?"

And he'd say something like, "Iran is nuts. You know what else is nuts? How tall Aaron is now. It is nuts!" I hope you people know that you are making us hate your kids. The way you incessantly blab about your fucking kid makes me dislike him just a little bit. It makes me hope that he ends up strung out on meth and robbing Laundromats for quarters. Would love to see that guy talk about Aaron if that happens. "Can you believe what's going on in Iran?" He'd probably say, "Iran? I know. You know who else ran? Aaron. From the cops. That kid is still wicked fast."

I swear some people become Stepford parents.

The worst are the parents who can't joke about their kids. I love my kids more than anything in the world. There isn't anything I wouldn't do for them. That being said, I also love making fun of them. Not just my kids, but other people's kids also. Not to their face, but behind their backs to other adults. There was a guy who used to coach a lot of kids' sports with me, and he was just like me. We would sit on the bench and insult all of them. "Look at Billy," he would say. "He has no idea where he is right now. He thinks he's at home eating a sandwich." It was our way of entertaining ourselves and getting out a little pent-up frustration.

One game, a woman in the stands heard what we were saying and afterward she approached us and said, "I want you to know that what you two were saying on the bench was extremely inappropriate."

Inappropriate. I hate that fucking word. That's the buzzword for what's good or not good for people under the age of seventeen.

"That movie is completely inappropriate for children."

"Those shorts are completely inappropriate."

"I can't allow my child to be around this language. It is completely inappropriate."

You know what's inappropriate? The fact that you can't laugh about how dopey your kid is. Just like all of us, they have good parts and bad parts. Of course, you should be proud if your son plays the shit out of a violin, but at the same time it's okay to acknowledge that he's probably a huge nerd who won't see a live naked woman until his first trip to Comic Con. The best parents see both sides and have fun with it. We freely admit that we love our kids more than anything in the world, and at the same time hate them and wish that they would move out of the house tomorrow.

I never really bought into any of the "now that you're a parent, things have to be different" shit. Sure, you can't go out until six in the morning, come home, and throw up on the couch but that doesn't mean you can't have fun. Good times do not have to end; you just have to pick and choose your spots. There were some other fathers at school who

I hung out with every now and then, and I knew from the stories they told that they had lived some pretty crazy lives prechildren. Every weekend one of them would say, "We should really just go away for a weekend. Vegas or something." Everyone would say, "Yeah" and "Definitely" but nobody would ever follow through. I was the only single guy in this group, so Vegas was an easy "yes" for me. I was also the only guy in that group who had less than a thousand dollars to his name, so Vegas was also an easy "no."

One Sunday, after a softball game, I was walking with one of the guys (let's just call him Jerry because that's his name) and he said, "Are you serious about Vegas? Because I am."

"Hell yeah, I'm serious," I said. "I'd go right now. I just don't have any money."

He put his softball gear in the back of his car and said, "If you can convince the other two (Gary and David) to go, arrange the hotel, and all that other shit, I'll cover your room, golf, and food. Deal?"

Fuck yeah, you have a deal. Are you kidding me? I hadn't been able to go to Vegas for years, and even though I wasn't going to be able to gamble and I didn't have enough money to even look at a lap dance, it still sounded like a pretty damn good time. Arranging the hotel and making a few dinner reservations was easy. Convincing the other two duds, er . . . dads was another story altogether.

I caught up with David at school one day and asked him point blank if he was serious about going to Vegas. "Are you kidding? I could never go. How am I going to get away?" he said.

"The same way Jerry and I are," I replied.

"You're single and Jerry's been married for twenty years. His wife doesn't give a shit what he does and he's got six kids. I don't even think he knows all of their names."

"I guarantee you that if you ask Lori [David's wife] if you can go to Vegas she'll say yes. No doubt in my mind."

"Whatever," he said. "I did Vegas with Lori and before Lori; there's nothing there for me anymore. I'm past that."

I couldn't believe it. Past Vegas? Past gambling, free booze, strip clubs, great golf, and phenomenal food? I understand feeling that way at a certain age but David was only thirty-five. There is no thirty-five-year-old male in the world who is past Vegas. They may think they are. They may have been told that they are. But deep down in their DNA, down in whatever piece of the molecular structure still allows some men to grow a full beard in half a day, down in that teeny, tiny collection of atoms that still allows ninety-five-year-old men to get boners, deep, deep, down there—there is a guy who wants to go to Vegas.

I feel I need to explain myself one more time. Because I picture people closing the book after that last paragraph and thinking, "What an asshole. If the guy doesn't want to go to Vegas, that's fine. It doesn't make him a loser. Maybe you're the loser. Did you ever think about that?"

Actually, I think about that all of the time. I think about the fact that I couldn't wait to get out of the house for a weekend of no responsibility. I think about the fact that I couldn't wait to get on the plane and order that first Jack and Coke. I think about the fact that I couldn't wait for the 5 AM Jack and Coke. I think the fact that I did think like that was actually *good* for my kids. I needed to recharge. Sitting in a tiny apartment with three kids all day can drive you loopy. You take a couple of days off and you come back better. Everyone needs a break sometimes from whatever they do.

A weekend away was going to do David some good even if he didn't know it.

A few of you are probably wondering, "Why didn't you just leave David home and go without him? Again, why do you have to be such an asshole?" Good question and I have a good answer for you. If David didn't go, Jerry wasn't going, and if Jerry wasn't going, there was nobody else around willing to float me a trip to Vegas. Were my reasons for making sure David went to Vegas selfish? Definitely. But I really did think it would do him a world of good.

Who am I kidding? I just wanted a free trip.

At one point David was Mr. Good Time. He was the guy that if nobody was up for going out, you knew David would be. I knew that guy was still in there somewhere and I also knew that there was only one person in the world who could find him.

His wife.

I saw her at school the next day and followed her into the parking lot. Lori hadn't forgotten how to have fun. She still did "girls' night" a couple of times a month, and was always popping out of town for a reunion or to reconnect with high school friends. Surely, she would understand.

"Hey, Lori, hold up. I have to ask you something," I said, walking after her.

"What's up?"

"We're thinking about going to Vegas for the weekend and we want to take David with us."

"Vegas? Are you kidding?" she said. Uh-oh. I guess I didn't read that one right. "He'll never go to Vegas. I can barely get him to leave the kids for a movie in town."

Or maybe I did.

"So you don't mind if he goes?" I asked.

"Are you kidding? He needs to go but he never will."

"So how do we make this happen?" I asked.

"I'll do it," she said, getting into her car. "But next time I get to go, too."

I had confidence that Lori would get the job done. One

down, one to go, and I knew this one wasn't going to be any easier.

Gary was a sports fanatic and a degenerate gambler. Hell, his bookie was a groomsman in his wedding. His love of betting also made him one of the most entertaining people in the world to be around because he basically "dared" people to do ridiculous shit for money. He would say things like, "I'll bet you $100 that that homeless guy is faster than you," and thirty seconds later you'd be racing a homeless person for a hundred bucks.

For the record, I lost that race.

We were in a mall once and he bet me fifty bucks that I couldn't hide from him for an hour. I hid, and he left, of course. Going out to lunch with Gary was an adventure because you just knew he was going to make one of the people he was with do something ridiculous. (I may or may not have eaten fifteen jelly packets in a minute for twenty dollars.)

Since Gary had his kid, the only sporty thing about him was the XXL Dodgers jersey that he wore every day to pick up his kid from school. What the hell happens to guys and what they decide is okay to wear after they have kids? I don't think I'm shocking anyone when I say that I'm no fashionista. Nobody has ever asked me what I'm "wearing" and every morning all I do is decide what color hoodie I want to put on that day. So I understand that maybe I shouldn't be the person who gets on other guys about what they wear, but...you'd have to hold me down and sedate me before I would wear shorts, black socks, and loafers. To me, the worst is the guy who hasn't bought any new "fancy" clothes in forever so when he goes out he's still wearing his shiny "go out shirt" and it's buttoned all the way to the top. Gary's fashion sense didn't say "athlete" or "old jock." It said, "I've given up. Please shoot me." Gentlemen, you are still being seen out in public, your wife still has to have sex with you, and sooner or later your kids are going to be old enough to realize that you are one embarrassing motherfucker. Get your shit together.

"Hey, man, you wanna go to Vegas with me, Jerry, and David?" I asked Gary as he was sitting in the pick-up line at school.

He stared straight ahead for a second. He had a look on his face as though I had mentioned a place he vaguely remembered from his youth, but he couldn't quite recall what it was like. He started to nod slowly. "Yeah, I'll go."

"Awesome."

The next day David called me and said, "I'm going to Vegas with you guys."

"Fantastic," I said.

"Not really. Lori's making me. I'm telling you, I really don't want to go. It's just not my thing anymore. The boys and I make dinner on the weekends for Lori and then we watch a movie on the couch until they go to sleep. And I'm going to miss that for what? It's just stupid."

I know some of you are thinking, "That's so sweet. He loves his family." And he really did. But he had lost his identity. If there's a parent out there who can look me in the eye and tell me with a hundred percent certainty that they want to be with their kids all of the time and they never want a break, I would tell you that I was looking in the eye of a bold-faced fucking liar. There is no way that's possible. *Nobody* is that interesting.

Do I think it's a good idea to go to Vegas with the guys every weekend if you're married with kids? No. Do I think it's a good idea to go to Vegas with the guys if you just had a kid? Probably not. Do I think that every now and then it's a good idea to get I-can't-remember-if-that's-water-or-piss-on-my-pants, I-know-I-wasn't-wearing-these-shoes-at-the-beginning-of-the-night, why-did-I-punch-that-cab-driver shitfaced in Vegas? Yes I do.

I made all of the hotel arrangements, set up some golf, made dinner reservations for Friday night, and counted down the days. I remember the very first time I left my kids. I was really nervous. I didn't think there was any way that they would survive without me. I remember pulling Trevor aside and having this big talk with him about how I was just a phone call away and that all of his uncles were there for anything he needed and that it was okay if he was sad because I was a little sad too. After I was done, he looked at me and said, "Can I go watch TV?"

That was the last time I was worried about going away.

I was lucky that I had all three of my brothers living in Los Angeles and available to babysit. The kids loved them and I trusted them. Except when there were diapers to be changed. I didn't really catch on to it at first. I would go out at night to do a set and my brother would come over to hang with the kids. Sometimes when I got back I would walk in and smell poop and my brother would tell me that it "just happened." Sometimes I'd walk in and the room would smell like someone had shit on some potpourri. I'd say, "What is that smell?" and he'd say, "I think he farted so I sprayed some freshener."

Eventually, my son figured out that when that one brother was there, his diaper was never going to get changed so he started holding it in until I got home. I would walk in the door and he'd look at me with sweat dripping off his forehead, his jaw clenched, just doing everything he could not to poop. You could see the relief on his face at the sight of me. "Thank God you're home! I didn't know how much longer I could hold it. I've been eating cheese for the last two hours to make sure there were no accidents."

The one thing about leaving my brothers with the kids was that there was always some surprise waiting for me when I got home. I'd walk in and my brother would grab his coat, head to the door, and say, "It was all good. We went to the park, did some swimming, rode our bikes. We did it all. Oh, your toilet shattered and all of the shelves in the refrigerator broke. I'll see you later." There was always something fucked up in my house when I left them. Always. I guess you get what you pay for.

When the Vegas weekend finally came, we flew out of Burbank on a Southwest flight. For those of you who have never been on a Southwest Airlines flight from Burbank to Vegas on a Thursday or Friday morning, let me just tell you that those flights are *packed* with strippers. Apparently, a lot of the strippers who work in Vegas don't live in Vegas. But, a lot of the strippers who work in Vegas do live in Burbank. We showed up at the airport and Gary was wearing his XXL Dodgers jersey and David was wearing a gray T-shirt with gray sweatpants, the ones with the elastic at the bottom.

"What do I care?" David said. "I'm not out looking for girls. It doesn't matter what I look like."

Maybe not to you but what about to the rest of us who have to look at you and walk with you through the airport? I've never understood that mentality. "It doesn't matter what I look like anymore—I'm married." With that kind of attitude you won't be married for long. I think it's mostly men who have that attitude. I travel a lot, and let me tell you that this country is filled with MILFs. It is truly impressive. Guys? Not so much. I did a show in Chicago last summer where I actually stopped in the middle to talk to a guy in the audience who was wearing a Bears jersey and sweatpants out on a date with his wife. He couldn't quite understand what the problem was. I pointed out that she was in amazing shape and he looked like he'd been eating butter straight out of the wrapper.

The flight is only forty-five minutes but apparently it was long enough for David to show pictures of his kids to the stripper he was sitting next to. It might have been the most embarrassing thing I have ever seen. Who in the world a) shows pictures of their kids to a complete stranger dressed in clear heels; b) shows pictures of his kids to someone after she offers him half off his first lap dance; and c) shows pictures of his kids to someone who said, "I coulda had two kids by now."

To say our first night in Vegas sucked would be a bit of an understatement. It licked donkey nuts. It might have been the single most disappointing night of my entire life. The plan when we landed was to go to the hotel, take a shower, grab some dinner, and then head out. Only one of those things happened because they all fell asleep. I couldn't believe it. And since I had no money, I was stuck in my room as well. I didn't even have any money to order porn or room service. Talk about an epic fail.

The next morning, when we met for breakfast, they all said the same thing: It had been so long since they had been in a quiet room by themselves they all masturbated and passed out. "I haven't seen porn in five years," Gary said. "I jerked off, passed out, woke up, did it again, and went back to sleep. Might have been one of the best nights of my life."

Lord, please don't ever let me end up like that. Please.

I could tell from the conversation that they were all thinking about doing some early-evening gambling so they could be back up in their rooms by ten to abuse themselves again. I couldn't believe that three grown men took a trip to Vegas to jerk off.

"Hey, we're going out tonight," I said. "There's no way we're having a repeat of last night."

"I'm not going to any dance scene or strip joint," David said. "If that's the plan, count me out."

"Dance scene or strip joint? Holy shit, how fucking old are you? I'm not saying anybody has to go anywhere they don't want to go, but we're in Vegas. Let's at least get drunk and have a good time."

Nothing.

I had to make sure that I didn't get stuck in my hotel room with no money again. "Gary, I'm broke. I'm not asking you to give me money; I'm asking you for the opportunity to earn some. You feel like making some bets?"

Gary smiled. "What kind of bets are we talking about?"

"I think you know. You pick the activity, I'll name what I think is a fair price, and we'll go from there."

Gary looked around and said, "So, for example, if I were to tell you that I would give you one hundred dollars to go up to that woman right there and pretend like someone paid you to do a singing strip-o-gram, what would you say?"

"I'd say, that's going to cost you two hundred and I have to be drunk."

Jerry smiled. "I remember this game."

I needed money because I wanted to gamble and head to a strip club, and the only way I was going to get it was to make a fool of myself for Gary's amusement. Golf was out because it was about 114 degrees, and the pool was out because Jerry said, "I ain't in the business of showin' nobody my bitch tits." Who can argue with that logic? We decided that we would go to one of those indoor racetracks where the go-carts can hit speeds of around sixty miles per hour. David was not going to go with us at first because he said, "It would be really irresponsible of me if something bad were to happen when I was out there." I had no idea he had turned into such a pussy. I actually suggested that he go into the steam room and just stay there until he died, but apparently he didn't think that was such a good idea. Jerry finally convinced him that coming with us was going to be more fun than hanging out by himself and he didn't have to get on the go-carts if he didn't want to.

When we got there, Gary said, "I'll give you fifty bucks if you do retarded boy for the whole time we're there." Retarded boy is pretty self-explanatory, I guess. Gary would pretend that he was my "handler" and I would act like I was a mentally retarded guy out for a day of fun. As we got older, we didn't do this gag much because not only was it in pretty poor taste but it was really hard to explain to people how you had become "unretarded" since the last time you saw them.

"Really?" I said. "We're jumping head first into retarded boy?"

"Why not?" he replied. "Might as well start out at the top."

Jerry seemed okay with it but David was not. "Guys, what if one of us had a mentally challenged child? How would you feel then?" What a stupid question. What a stupid fucking question and it's one that I hate more than anything. Of course nobody is wishing anything bad on anyone else. Of course our intent is not to be mean or hateful. But I come from a train of thought where it's okay to make fun of pretty much anything. It's all about intent. And our intention with retarded boy, and any of our stupid jokes, was to make each other laugh and to make other people uncomfortable. That's it. To all of you people who say you have never made a joke that was "insensitive," I would tell you that you are full of shit. Jokes are jokes. Deal with it.

When I was Retarded Boy, my name was Raymond.

"Raymond," Gary said. "Do you want to drive a car?"

"They go fast, Gary! They go really fast!" I said.

"Yes, they do. Do you want to drive one?" he said loud enough for the person working the counter to hear.

"Yes! Yes, yes, yes! I'm gonna drive one of them fast cars."

Gary walked up to the counter and said, "Can we get six races?"

"How many drivers?" the counter guy said nervously.

"Uh...me, Jerry, and him." Gary pointed at me as I waved.

"Yeah, uh, every driver needs a driver's license, so..." the kid responded.

"That's not a problem. Guys, lemme see your licenses."

I handed him my license and said, "Not a problem!"

The counter guy was fucking stunned. He kept looking at my ID and looking at me and looking at the picture and then back at me. "Is...is...is he allowed to drive?" the kid asked Gary.

"He's got a license. He can drive."

"But...uh...he's..." the kid stammered.

"He's what? Retarded? Are you saying you have a no-retarded-person policy here at this establishment?" Gary asked.

"I wanna drive, Gary. You said I could drive!" I screamed.

At this point, this poor kid didn't know what the fuck to do. Common sense told him there was no way I should be driving but my driver's license told him something completely different. On top of that, we were starting to make a bit of a scene. "No, no, no. That's not what I'm saying at all. If you guys say he's safe to drive, I mean, he has a license, right?"

My biggest problem when I was Raymond was not laughing. So, when I felt I was going to, I'd make really loud whooping noises. "Whoop! Whoop! We're going driving! We're going driving!" Jerry was hiding in a corner trying not to laugh and David had walked clear to the other side of the building so he wouldn't have to be involved.

The kid gave me *the biggest* helmet I have ever seen. It was freakin' gigantic. I don't think I could have hurt my head if I had fallen out of a plane with no parachute. My neck almost wasn't strong enough to hold it up.

By the time we got out on the track, everyone in there had gathered around to see the mentally retarded man drive. Some people requested not to drive at the same time as I did and some people actually wanted to. There were a few college aged kids, who decided to race at the same time, and I heard them making fun of me.

That's where I draw the line. I would never make fun of a retarded person. I know some of you may be confused because I was walking around acting retarded, but to me, that is completely different. We were doing something for our entertainment. I would never ridicule someone for a malady. I totally get that some people may see this as a blurry, morally bankrupt line and I respect that. To me, those kids were making fun of a fake retarded person to his face and that was not okay. It was time to set them straight.

As Jerry was getting me in my ride, I whispered to him, "How funny would it be if Raymond won?"

"Pretty damn funny," he said.

I looked around and there was a pretty big crowd watching the race. I couldn't believe it. We had never made Raymond good at anything before. This was a new twist and I liked it.

"Kick their ass!" one guy called out to me.

"You're gonna do great!" another guy called out.

"I'm thirsty!" I called back and gave everyone two thumbs up.

For whatever reason, I always made Raymond thirsty. Don't ask me why.

When I tell you that I drove better than I had ever driven before, it is no exaggeration. Not only did I finish first by a lot, but not one of those little assholes even finished the race. One got kicked off for swearing at me and the other one, the real doucheface who was stuttering and crossing his eyes at me, got out of his go-cart at one point and was hit by some guy behind him who was flying around a corner. Karma is a bitch. I sure hope it doesn't come back to bite me because of Raymond.

It was only one o'clock and I had already made fifty bucks. I wanted to make five hundred by ten that night. I figured that was just enough money to get me into some trouble. Gary was ready to have some more fun. I told him my goal and he just smiled and said, "This is gonna be a great night." If I remember correctly, that day I walked through the casino in Speedos ($20); I asked a woman who was clearly not a hooker how much for a "date" and would she be open to a two-handed prostate massage ($50 and I got punched in the chest); I exited a bathroom stall with chocolate smeared all over my hands and then used the sink/towel dispenser and left chocolate all over the bathroom ($40 and one of the funniest things ever); I went up to a guy who was with a group of his buddies and pretended to be his gay lover whom he never called anymore ($100 and I know it seems like a lot but any joke where there's a chance of bodily harm costs more); and to end the afternoon I did my singing strip-o-gram to a seventy-year-old woman who was eating an early dinner (should have been $200 but Gary gave me $240). The best part about that was that her husband pretended he had ordered it for her.

By this time, Jerry, Gary, and I were all shitfaced and David was just being Debbie Downer. "Just go up to your room and jerk off if you're gonna be like this all night, David," I said as I returned from giving a lap dance to a senior citizen. "You're ridiculous."

"Well, excuse me if I don't find this fun anymore. I didn't want to come, remember?"

"Have one drink. Just have one drink, and then we can eat some dinner and you can go to your room."

He stared at us for a beat. "One drink and that's it."

I don't know about you but I can't have just one drink. People ask me all the time why I don't have drinks with dinner. Because I can't have just one drink. Why don't I have a cocktail at my house? Because I can't have just one drink. Apparently, David was the same way.

Wow.

As soon as that first drink hit his lips, he was a different person. "Man, this beer tastes good! Lemme get another."

Okay.

When that beer was done... "Let's do some shots! Who wants shots?" And just like that, Good Time Guy was back. From that point on, the night became one of the truly greatest nights of my life. That night was actually the genesis of my favorite game to play in Vegas even to this day: Spot the Hooker. David came up with it and the name pretty much explains what it is but maybe I should give a few details. Basically, you stand at one of the casino bars and, duh, try and guess which girls are "working." When you find one who you're sure is on the clock, you walk up to her and ask her for a "date." If you're right, your next drink is free. If you're wrong, well, just imagine what you would do if someone walked up to you (or your girlfriend/wife/friend) and asked you how much it would cost to take you upstairs to have sex.

I ended up being pretty good at the game because I started to notice some very consistent telltale signs: small purse, sipping on the same drink for a long time, wandering eye, noncomplicated clothing, and, as you got later in the night, wrinkled dresses and fucked-up hair. It was ironic that I was so good at spotting them because I was the only one in the group who had never been with one before. I know, I know. "But, Josh, you seem like the kind of guy who has had sex with tons of hookers." Thank you. That's too kind. (I really have to check what I'm putting out there because everyone thinks the same thing.) It's never appealed to me at all. I know some people think, "Well, you like strip clubs. Same thing, right?" Not. At. All. The thing that has never appealed to me about hookers is the idea of paying for it. That makes it a business transaction and

117

what I enjoyed more than anything when I was out meeting women was the sport of it. That's why strip clubs were so appealing to me. There was a sense that I was competing against every other guy in there for that one girl, and even though nobody else knew there was a competition, it didn't matter because I did. I do the same thing on the freeways. I race people who have no idea they are in a race. It keeps things interesting.

The guys refused to believe that I had never been with a pro before. "It's never happened before and it's never going to happen," I said. "I really have no interest at all."

Gary smiled. "Five hundred bucks says you will."

Well, shit. Five hundred bucks? At that time, five hundred dollars was almost two weeks' worth of money. Five hundred dollars would mean a very "special" trip to In-N-Out with the kids. Five hundred dollars meant I had to have sex with a woman.

"Okay," I said. "Let me go pick one out."

"Not so fast," Gary said. "You don't get to pick her out. We do."

Uh-oh. That didn't sound very promising. The problem with my buddies being in charge of ordering the girl was that they had the same sense of humor as I did—sick. If I were them, I would have gone for the joke. It's one of the reasons people stopped asking me to plan bachelor parties, because I went for the joke.

Knowing what would happen if I let them pick the hooker I said, "No fucking way. There is no way in the world I'm letting you guys pick."

"Okay, relax, *relax*," Gary said. "Look, I'm not going to let you pick what you want because that would be no fun for me, but you always have the option to say no, so let's just nose around and see what we can come up with. Deal?"

That sounded fair enough. All I had to do was say no if I didn't want to do it. Looking back, I see how Gary was really smart about the way he did this. He was a pro and I only thought I was. He went outside and got a shitload of hooker menus and every twenty minutes or so we would look at one just to see what they were offering. In between looking, he was feeding me drinks and making it seem like he wasn't even that interested. A couple of times, he waited so long in between looking, I actually reminded him about the bet.

By midnight, I was really drunk and he started in on my manhood. Damn you testosterone! "Look, I don't even know what the big deal is," he said. "Any single guy I know would do it for free just for the story, but throw in five hundred dollars? The more I think about it, the more I think this is a bad deal for me."

In my drunken stupor, not only was he making me feel like a pussy but he was preying on my financial vulnerability. He was truly The Master. "Fine! I'll do it!" I said. "You narrow it down to three and I'll pick from there."

He must have known the psychological warfare had been working because he had a list ready: an amputee, a dominatrix, and a giant Puerto Rican.

Right away, I told him there was no chance of the dominatrix. Not my thing at all. That quickly, choices were narrowed down to an amputee and a giant Puerto Rican.

"She's only missing one leg," he said. "It's nothing crazy." Easy for him to say.

"How big is the Puerto Rican?" I asked.

"I asked the same question," he said. "Apparently, she's not fat. She's just big."

"Why'd she make the list then?"

"I've never seen a giant Puerto Rican before. Just wanted to know what they looked like."

To me, there wasn't even a question of who I was choosing. After calling for the giant Puerto Rican, we all went up to my room to wait for her and have some more drinks. If I was doing this, I was going to have to be completely wasted. An hour went by and Jerry and Gary both fell asleep, but no Puerto Rican. Another thirty minutes went by and I fell asleep but still no Puerto Rican. I don't know how long I had been sleeping but I woke up to David leaning over me and whispering, "She's here."

I opened my eyes and saw that Gary and Jerry were still sleeping.

"Do you want to answer the door or do you want me to?" David asked.

"Did you fall asleep too?" I asked.

"Are you kidding? This might be the greatest story of all time. There was no way I was going to sleep through it," David said, as he took another sip from a beer.

Knock-knock.

"Don't answer it," I said. Why couldn't I just tell Gary that he had slept through the whole thing? All I had to do was convince David to go along with the story and at this point of the evening—that seemed easy enough. "David, you wanna fuck with Gary?"

David smiled but before he could say anything...

"You can fuck with me all you want after you answer the door," Gary said with his eyes still closed. "I can pretend to be asleep for only so long."

"Me, too," said Jerry.

David smiled even wider.

Knock-knock.

"Fine! I'll do it," I said. "But after I answer the door, you guys have got to get the fuck out of here."

"Not a chance," said Gary. "It's my money. I'm sticking around to make sure you live up to your end of the bet." And he closed his eyes to pretend he was asleep again.

I told David and Jerry that they had to go as soon as she came in but they both said there was no way that was happening as they walked into the bathroom and closed the door.

Knock-knock.

Shit. I took a deep breath, walked to the door, and opened it. I know a lot of people get accused of false advertising. Maybe the car they're selling wasn't "mint," or maybe the gym equipment they're trying to unload wasn't "just like new" but that was not the case here. This woman was truly a giant Puerto Rican. She must have been 6'4".

"I thought you had forgotten about me," she said.

I really wished I had.

She walked into the room. "Is your friend joining us?"

"No. He's passed out."

"Okay, but if I even see him open his eyes it's extra. This ain't no peep show," she said as she surveyed the room. "A couple of things you need to know. First of all, I am not a man; you'll see that soon enough." Phew. That was actually going to be my first question. "Second, your time starts now and you have an hour to do what you need to do. You can come only once. Once you're done, I'm done, unless you feel like paying for another hour. Next, we can kiss but we don't have to…"

Wait, wait, wait. Who the hell kisses a hooker? Is that really a thing? Deeeeeeeesgusting.

"...there is no doggy style—"

"Hold on. Just out of curiosity, why is there no doggy style?" I asked.

"Because I don't want you taking off your rubber?"

Wait, wait, wait. Who the hell takes off their rubber when they're having sex with a hooker? Deeeeeeeees-gusting.

"If you don't have any other questions, let's get this started," she said as she took out a timer and put it on the table. This was the worst, and exactly what I always thought I would hate about a prostitute—it was all business. She put a timer on the table like I was making hard-boiled eggs! She slipped off her dress, said, "If I'm standing, it's extra" and lay down on the bed.

If someone said to me, "Josh, at one point in your life, when you aren't sure if you're going to be able to make rent every month, somebody is going to pay you $500 to have sex with a very attractive, albeit large, Puerto Rican woman and not only will you never have to see her again but it will be one of the greatest stories of all time," I would have told you that sounds like the best deal ever.

But for some reason this wasn't.

"I can't do this. You're gonna have to leave," I said. "Sorry."

"You are the biggest pussy in the entire world," Gary said, sitting up. "Just do it."

"I told you it's extra if he opened his eyes. That's extra," the giant said.

"It's not extra because we're not doing anything," I said. She said she wasn't leaving until she got some money for her time and finally left only after Gary gave her $200.

On her way out, she left us with this little gem: "You know when I said I'm not a man? Well, I used to be. Does that change anything?"

"I'll give you one thousand dollars to have sex with her now!" Gary screamed at me.

No, thank you.

When we got back to Los Angeles, David invited all of us to his house for a party the next weekend. He actually told me that going to Vegas was the best thing that had happened to his marriage because he "remembered David." In order to be a good parent or husband, I truly believe that you have to have your own identity. You can't live your life through other people. Even if that means coming face to face with a giant Puerto Rican every now and then.

P.S. I don't know what it is about Vegas that makes men want to go to a strip club but it's very real. Hell, it's not just men. Places like Thunder Down Under and Chippendales are packed there too. I went to one of those places once. I was dating a girl who went to a strip club with me, so one night she made me go to a male nude place with her. Uh, women go fucking wacko in those places.

In the places I'm used to going to, guys just stare at the stage like they've been dosed with lithium. There's barely any talking. It's just a bunch of dudes who don't have to pretend that they're not looking at boobies anymore. I know some people think those places are sad but they're really not. And I know some people think those places are horrible because women are objectified and degraded, and I couldn't disagree more. If you've ever been in one of those places, you'd know that the men aren't the predators; the women are. We aren't the lions out on the Serengeti looking for food; it's the women who stalk those places looking for prey. It's the women who are looking for the drunkest and the stupidest one of us to track down and fill full of lies about how much they like us and how they would definitely go home with us if they weren't working. It's the women who spin the stories about how different we are from the rest and how they've never been able to talk to anyone else like this before. It's the women who are in control. No doubt at all that they are driving that bus and taking it anywhere they want while we ride in the back, looking like someone who just lost their ability to think or walk. I understand that some of the women who are performing at these establishments aren't the most mentally stable people in the world but, who is?

The male nude places aren't like that at all. When the men walk out on stage, women lose their fucking minds. Screaming, grabbing, and clawing like the guy is just some piece of meat who was thrown into the cage at feeding time. When I went, I couldn't believe what those guys had to put up with. One of the guys fell into the crowd and came out looking like he had been thrown out of a moving car.

P.P.S. The last bachelor party somebody asked me to plan was in Seattle, and I called a woman whose classified ad read, "I'll wrestle you..." Her deal was that she came over, got naked, and threw people around for half an hour. How did she throw people around, you ask? She was 6'1", 220 pounds, that's how. I had hired a stripper also but I thought we'd bring out the wrestler first to really get the party started. We blindfolded my buddy, sat him down on a chair in the living room, and asked him if he was ready.

"I'm so ready for this," he said. "You have no idea."

Yes, I did. As a matter of fact, I was looking forward to it more than he was. I wish I could explain the look on my friend's face when he saw this giant naked woman standing in front of him because it truly was something I'd never seen before. He didn't take his eyes off her and all he said was, "Why did you do this?"

After that, the woman basically beat the shit out of him with her titties and sat on his head for thirty minutes. It was an awesome experience and one I highly recommend to anyone planning a bachelor party and willing to lose a friend. I didn't actually lose him as a friend and he did get me back by putting a fucking snake in my bed. I have to admit, the video from that was hilarious. I screamed like an eight-year-old, leaped out of my bed, and ran into the closed door. Not my finest hour.

CHAPTER 6

Your Son Is Not Derek Jeter

Y our son is not going to play professional baseball.
Too harsh? Well, guess what? Your daughter isn't
playing on the U.S. women's soccer team either.

It really is amazing to see so many delusional people
out at the park on the weekends with their kids. Do they
have any idea of the difference between professional athletes and the rest of us? Do they go around saying Lindsay
Lohan is as smart as Albert Einstein because she also has
a brain?

A guy recently told me that his son had "a major league
arm." His seven-year-old son. Major league arm. I
watched the kid throw and the only thing major league
about him was the hat he was wearing. He looked like a
newborn calf that had been oxygen deprived and could see
out of only one eye. He could barely throw the ball to his
father but the guy kept saying, "You see that? You see how

much that ball drops?" It's dropping because that's what balls do when you throw them. And speaking of balls dropping, you might want to wait until your son's balls do the same before you start crowning him the next Babe Ruth.

I love baseball. Probably a little too much, if you ask my wife. The worst thing that ever happened to our marriage was the baseball package on DirecTV. Every hit, every pitch, every inning on my TV in my living room is like a seven-month death march for my marriage. Somehow we make it through every year, but barely.

And don't think about talking to me during a Red Sox–Yankees game or I will lose my shit. When Jacob was young, we were watching a game and there was a call I didn't like so I screamed, "You have got to be kidding me! That's bullshit!" I looked over at him and I could see he was scared. I'm not a yeller at all, so when I raise my voice, it means something is really wrong.

"Are you okay, buddy?" I asked.

"You're scaring me," he said.

I felt horrible that he had seen me scream like that so I leaned over to him and said, "If you didn't like that you should probably go upstairs because there's going to be a lot more where that came from."

You didn't think I was going to stop yelling at the TV, right? Either get on board or jump ship because that's pretty much how I roll with all of my teams. I should clarify a few things, though. Yes, I yell at the TV, and yes, I have been known to stay in a certain seat on the couch and never move if my team is doing well. But I have never, I repeat never, painted my face for a game. I have never, I repeat never, worn an authentic jersey to a game (not since I was fourteen anyway). I don't have a man cave, I've never gotten into a fight over a sporting event, I've never named one of my kids after an athlete or a team, and, although I do have tattoos, I would never tattoo the name of a team or a team logo onto my body. Yes, I'm a sports fanatic but I'm not an idiot and, most important, I like vagina and I don't think I would ever see one again if I did do any of the those things.

Jacob is the only one of my kids who truly caught the sports bug from me. About a year after I scared him off the couch he started joining in on the screaming. Not my proudest moment but pretty damn close. As much as I like watching my teams play, though, I like watching Jacob play sports more. His main sport is baseball (thank God) and he pretty much likes playing all sports except soccer (thank God). He played one year of soccer when he was seven. He never said much about it until the final game. The whistle blew, and he walked off the field, took off his shirt, and said, "I am never playing this sport again."

I've coached or helped coach most of his teams but my

"expertise" is in baseball. I played college baseball so I like to think that I know a lot, but the truth is, almost every father I've ever met on the baseball field thinks he knows a lot too. And I'm not going to lie—I always tried to win. Some people say, "It doesn't matter if you win or lose as long as you're having fun." I would ask those people what's more fun: winning or losing? I guarantee that if you went up to the team that got their dicks knocked in the dirt and asked every single kid on the team if they had fun, they would say no.

On the other hand, you can't be the guy who makes eight-year-olds run wind sprints at noon in the middle of July. I always made sure I was somewhere in the middle. The kids on my teams loved coming to practice and we kept things positive. At the same time, if you sucked, you weren't playing shortstop. Or pitcher. Or anywhere the ball might find you.

The worst thing about coaching is the fathers who can't give up the dream and insist that their little boy is going to play baseball. One kid used to show up to practice in a tutu because he would come there from ballet class. His father would tell me, "He's trying to decide between ballet and baseball right now." Uh...no, he's not. I've known a lot of guys who played baseball and I have never met one who couldn't decide if he wanted to be Barry Bonds or Billy Elliot. But this father would not give up the dream.

I was really impressed with this kid (Benny) because at eight, he knew who he was. He didn't want to wear cleats on the field, liked his slippers, wouldn't wear the glove because it made his hands sweat, and liked to sit out in the outfield and pick flowers. When the ball would get hit to him he ran away from it screaming, "Somebody come get it! I don't want it!" I know you shouldn't label an eight-year-old child as gay but if the ballet shoe fits ... I've actually run into the kid since then and, at seventeen, he is out, loud, and proud.

Benny and I had an understanding. He hated being on the field but he wouldn't complain or cause any trouble, and I played him only when I had to and basically left him alone to pick flowers and catch butterflies. The catching butterflies used to drive his father crazy! I think Benny did it just to bother him. I say this because I know for a fact that Benny *hated* to sweat.

He'd say, "Coach Wolf, I don't understand why you have to play baseball when it's so hot. I can feel sweat on my back. Is it okay if I don't move?" And he wouldn't move for the rest of the game. But when he started chasing those butterflies, man oh man, did he get those little legs pumping. And the louder his father yelled, "Benny, leave those butterflies alone! Leave them alone!" the faster Benny would run.

Sometimes while chasing butterflies Benny would do

those things that ballet dancers do where they look like gazelles bounding across a field. Hold on while I look that up ... *Grand jeté* is what it's called. In the middle of an inning, he would chase butterflies around the outfield doing *grand jetés* and it was one of the funniest things I have ever seen.

His dad would lose his fucking mind. "Pull him out of the game."

"Why?" I would ask.

"Because he's prancing in the outfield. You're not allowed to prance in the outfield."

I actually called time out once, walked to the umpire, and said, "Is there a rule against a player on the field chasing a butterfly?"

Umpires who work at the park are either fourteen-year-old pimply kids or eighty-five-year-old guys who have a hard time not pooping during the game. Neither has any clue about the rules of the game or really seems to care that much. In this case, the ump was a kid and he said, "Dude, I don't care what he does. I just want this game to be over with."

One day after my brother saw Benny in action, he asked me, "What would you do if your son was gay?"

I've always said that I just want my kids to pick something they love and to be the best at it. I think that if your kids do that, they'll be happy. That means if my son was gay, I would want him to suck the best dick this side of the Mississippi. I would want him driving a convertible yellow Miata wearing a "Shut up and dance" T-shirt. *Soooooooooooo* gay. When he takes his phone out of his pocket, I want dicks to fall out. Gay. Benny and his father left the park for good after Benny turned ten. He finally caught a butterfly and was happier than I had ever seen him. "I caught it! I can't believe I actually caught it! Dad, look!" He started running toward the bleachers with this huge smile on his face. This was his moment. For four years, he had been chasing butterflies and had never even come close to one and today was his home run trot, his bases loaded, two-out hit that won his team the game.

But on his way to share his triumph with his father, he tripped and landed hands first. When he lifted his hand and saw the butterfly smushed against his palm, he started flopping around on the ground like a fish and making high-pitched dolphin noises. We ran out to try to calm him down but there wasn't a chance in hell of that happening. At one point, he actually pretended he was dead. He let his body go limp and didn't respond to anything or anybody until his father sat down next to him and said, "Benny, look what I've got for you. Benny."

No response.

"It's too bad Benny's dead because he'll never get to see this butterfly I caught for him."

One of Benny's eyes flickered open and, sure enough, his father was holding a butterfly. "Where did you get that?" Benny asked.

"You looked like you were having so much fun, I thought I'd join in," his father responded. It was the last baseball game Benny ever played.

That actually never happened.

Are you kidding me? What really happened was this.

His father came out on the field wearing god-awful spandex shorts, knelt down next to Benny, and said, "Get up, Benny. We know you're not dead."

And then I heard the funniest thing I have ever heard in my life. The one thing that makes me laugh whenever I'm at my lowest.

"Excuse me, Benny's daddy," my son said. "I can see your penis." Sure enough, his spandex shorts had a tiny tear in them and a little bit of the mushroom was sprouting out.

"I've never seen a penis when I was playing baseball before," another one of the kids said.

That got everyone, including Benny, laughing uncontrollably. His dad was incredibly embarrassed, scooped Benny up, and we never saw either one of them at the park again.

And then there was one year that I talked my oldest son, Trevor, into playing baseball and it turned out to be the most memorable summer of my life. I was living in Hollywood at the time and, since I didn't have a job or any money, we spent a shitload of time at the park. Trevor was a great athlete, but wasn't the most socially gifted kid in the world. I thought that being on a team would be good for him. One summer wouldn't kill him and maybe he would end up loving it.

I went down to the park to sign him up. The guy in the office told me that it was too late to sign up because try-outs had already happened but maybe Trevor could get on a team if I volunteered to coach. I loved that idea. Not only did I dig coaching but this way I could guarantee that Trevor had a good experience. Was that cheating? Of course it was. Parenting is hard enough so I cheat whenever I can.

"Great. Come back on Monday and we'll set you up."

"But I didn't see the kids' tryout. How am I going to draft them?"

"It'll be fine. We'll make it work. Trust me."

If I've learned anything in this life it's to never, ever, ever believe any motherfucker who says, "Trust me." Only in a Bruce Willis movie from the eighties is that good and only if Bruce is the guy saying it. Trust me? The person who's saying that might as well be saying, "I am going to fuck you over like nobody has ever been fucked over before."

"I've never done this before." Trust me.

"I forgot my wallet at my house." Trust me.

"You'll be there for only an hour." Trust me.

"You're going to love her. She looks just like Cindy Crawford." Trust me.

"Can I borrow $100? I'll have it back in a week." Trust me.

I went back in a week, walked into the office, and the guy handed me a piece of paper that had my team's roster on it.

I looked at the team and noticed a definite trend. More than half of the names on the list were Russian.

"We didn't want to break them up," he explained. "A few of the parents don't speak English so we wanted to keep them all together."

Huh.

"Oh, and you got the Gonzalez twins too. They don't speak English that well either but the father is willing to help out at practice."

But…

"Here's your equipment." He put a bag at my feet. "Because you guys were a last-minute team, there are only two batting helmets right now but we'll try and find you a few more before the season starts."

Wait, wait, wait. Last-minute team?

As you can imagine, the first practice was amazing.

And by amazing, I mean my guys made up the single

worst collection of baseball players I had ever seen in one place. Jerry's Kids would have made a better squad. If you had put out an ad for the worst baseball players in the world who knew nothing about the game and listed English as their second language, you still wouldn't have come up with this group. That was the bad part. The good part was that I love a train wreck and I could see this one coming from miles away. On top of that, and most important, my son was excited about playing. As soon as he found out we were on a team, he put eye black on every morning to get ready for the season. There was no backing out now.

The first people to show up for practice were the Gonzalez twins. I was actually happy that they were the first kids there because it gave me a minute to talk to their father. *"Da me una cerveza,"* *"Donde estan los baños como los que encuentran en los Estados Unidos?"* and *"Cuanto para otro baile?"* were the extent of my Spanish. There was no way I would be able to tell those kids what I needed them to do without the help of their father.

I walked up to him, held out my hand, and said, "I'm Josh. I'm coaching the team. I heard you were willing to help out and I really appreciate that. Not only would it be impossible to run practice by myself but I don't speak Spanish so I'm going to have to rely on you to talk with your kids."

He just stared at me and smiled.

I knew that stare. I had seen it many times before when I was talking to nannies in the park. Me talking to him was like when I watch Telemundo and I pick up only every tenth word. He didn't speak English for shit so I tried again but this time in a way more embarrassing way.

Loud and slow: "Are you here to help me coach?"

When someone doesn't speak English, not only do I talk to them like they're deaf but I also end up doing it with some horrible version of their accent. I catch myself doing it all of the time in sushi restaurants when I order the "clab lorr."

And then the Russian floodgates opened. I couldn't believe what I was seeing. The kids wore jeans with black loafers, only a few of them had gloves and all of the fathers were wearing track suits with no underwear. When the entire team got there, I lined them up and these were the highlights.

Simon (Russian) was a short fat kid who never stopped talking but was funny as shit.

Victor (Russian) had never played baseball before but was a fantastic athlete and his father was a dentist (more on that later).

Ivan (Russian) had never played baseball and was way, way, way into hip-hop culture.

Jorge and Rodrigo Gonzalez (Mexican) had never left each other's side and didn't speak English.

Gregory (black) was an enormous kid with zero coordination and as gentle a kid as I have ever met in my life.

Geoffrey (Asian) never looked up from the ground and I wasn't sure if he had a voice box.

My son, Trevor (white), who had been spitting sunflower seeds in my apartment for two weeks in preparation for the season.

For me to say these kids were bad would be like saying Hurricane Katrina made it kinda rain. The only bright spot was Victor. Sure he was wearing his glove on the wrong hand for the first fifteen minutes but when he switched glove hands... Wow. He had an amazing arm.

After practice, I spoke with Victor's father for a few minutes and found out that he was a dentist. It didn't make a whole lot of sense because both he and Victor were missing teeth. It's like having a fat trainer at the gym. Doesn't exactly fill you with confidence. He couldn't guarantee that Victor would be there at every game or practice because he was his dental assistant.

Excuse me? Can you imagine going to a dentist to get your wisdom teeth out and the dentist is missing teeth and his assistant is eleven? There isn't enough laughing gas in the world.

I also had a chance to speak to Gregory's parents for

a little bit. Both his father and mother were big, athletic people. His dad had played in the NFL and his mother had run track in college. How these athletic machines spawned a kid who hit himself in the face with the ball when he was playing catch (it happened and to this day I'm not sure how) was beyond me.

When we got home, I thought my son would be upset. I expected him to give the whole "We suck!" speech and I wouldn't have been able to tell him he was wrong. I've never been the guy to lie to my kids about things like that. What's the point? I'm not an asshole but I don't blow smoke up their ass either. If he had asked me if the team was bad I would have said yes.

But if I told Trevor the honest truth about our team, it would ruin the whole summer for him. Couldn't risk it, not for his own good. So—and I'm not proud of this—I pretty much baited him into an argument and sent him to his room for the night.

I never said I was perfect.

At the second practice, I went over to speak with Ivan and this kid made the rest of them seem boring. He was a white, pasty-pale Russian with one of those typical big Russian block heads. No mistaking where he came from but he wasn't having any of it.

"Yo, wha's up, Wolfie-Wolf?" he said. He went on to tell me he was sure that he had been adopted and that he

knew deep down that he was half black. He called everyone "white boy" and would show up to practice wearing
chains, rings, sunglasses, the whole deal. It was the single
most ridiculous thing I had ever seen. Even more ridiculous was that he wouldn't answer to Ivan. We had to call
him Poison Ivy.

Before our first game, I checked in with Trevor. The
team was pretty cliquey and he didn't exactly fit in with
anyone. "You ready for today, buddy?"

"I guess so," he said.

"Just go out there and do your best. That's all you can
do."

"Okay." Beat. "Hey, Dad?"

"Yeah."

"Is it true you get ice cream after every game? Because
Kaitlynn said it wasn't and I said it was."

Damn you, Kaitlynn, and your truth telling!

"Maybe not after every game but we'll get some after
today's game for sure." He was going to need some
cheering up after the complete beating we were about to
take.

The other team ran out on the field and right away I
knew we were in trouble. They were all athletes, all Mexican, and all business. They had been playing together
since they were six years old and they talked to each other
only in Spanish, yelling plays and signs so we had no idea

what they were saying. I tried asking Rodrigo and Jorge to translate but they just smiled at me.

The game was called in the second inning and we lost twenty-seven-to nothing.

I took Trevor out for ice cream after the game. Midway through his mint chocolate chip cone he said to me, "I don't get it."

"What don't you get, T?"

"I don't get why you like baseball so much. It's hot and boring."

I started to wonder if I had made a mistake having him play. I wanted him to look back on playing baseball with the same sense of nostalgia that I did. I definitely didn't want to ruin it for him. I wasn't sure what to do but I knew I had to make it more fun.

I knew a single mother who was a sales rep for Otis Spunkmeyer cookies and she always had a trunk full of samples. I thought I would use the cookies as rewards.

At practice, I gave a cookie for everything. Cookie for the longest ball, cookie for the most hits, cookie for the group that struck out the least, cookie for Gregory if he didn't hit himself with the bat, cookie, cookie, cookie. For the first time, they looked like they were having fun. They still sucked, but they were having fun. By the end of practice everyone had had at least one cookie except Simon, who started screaming, "What's a fat kid gotta do

143

to get a freakin' cookie?" Turns out all he had to do was say that.

When the second game rolled around, we still sucked the big one, and on top of that Poison Ivy almost got us killed.

He was on first base and the first baseman for the other team was black. Poison Ivy decided to ask the kid who his favorite rapper was and when the kid gave him an answer he didn't like, Poison Ivy said, "Pffffff. Nigga, please."

I don't know how to write the sound of a needle being scratched off a record player and I don't know if some of you reading this book even know what a record is, but trust me, when it happens, nothing good follows.

"What did you say?" the kid said, amazed.

"Don't be like that, my brother," Poison Ivy returned. "It's all good." And he put his hand out to shake.

The black kid slapped his hand down and said, "It's definitely not all good." Then he screamed across to his side of the field. "Hey! This kid just called me a nigger!"

Uh-oh.

But it got worse.

Poison Ivy started screaming, "I am a nigger! I am a nigger!"

Pretty soon we had the first baseman's family and friends running out onto the field, and from our side a bunch of middle-aged Russian men in tracksuits started making their way from the stands. It looked like we were going to have a full-on brawl until Gregory's father stepped in. Gregory's dad was a big, big man. He stepped right in the middle of that clusterfuck, pulled the black kid's family aside, and told them the truth.

"Look," he said. "I know you're mad. So am I. The truth is that kid actually thinks he's half black."

"What are you talking about?" the first baseman's father said. "He's Russian!"

After about ten minutes, the tension went away and we got back to playing the game. We lost seventeen to two. Over the next two weeks, we continued to lose but we also kept getting better. The kids were scoring runs, we were teaching Victor how to pitch, and Poison Ivy hadn't started a race riot. When the fifth game rolled around, I could tell something was going to be different. The kids scored two runs in the first inning. I couldn't believe it. Our first lead of the year! I was trying to figure out a way to stall so we could end the game in the first inning but outside of Poison Ivy yelling out more racist stuff, I couldn't come up with anything.

And then something happened.

Victor threw strike one.

Victor threw strike two.

And then Victor threw strike three.

I couldn't believe what I saw. Victor looked at me and

said, "I think I figured it out." And he had. He was absolutely amazing and we won. And we won again. Then we won again. And then we won again. I could not believe what was happening. It was like the real-life *Bad News Bears* but with a Russian accent.

We had two games left and all we had to do was win one of them and we were going to make the playoffs. Easy, right? Nope. As we were getting warmed up for our next game, Simon ran up to the field and said, "Coach, Victor's not coming anymore."

"Why not? Is he okay?" I asked.

"He's fine. It's just that his dad needs him to help him at the office. Victor's been here so much that his dad's losing money with his business."

Shit.

Needless to say we lost.

"There's no way we win the next game without Victor," Simon said on the bench after the game. The other kids agreed. Shit, I agreed, too. We were one win away from the playoffs and I was going to do whatever I could to make sure Victor made it to the next game.

Later that afternoon, Trevor and I went over to Victor's apartment to see if we could talk his father into letting him play for a few more weeks. There was no way in the world I could have been prepared for what I was about to see.

Trevor and I had been having one of those father-son talks where the dad thinks he's imparting some sage, life-changing advice and the son is just wondering when the fuck the father is going to shut up. I know when my kids are thinking it but I can never stop myself! When we got to their apartment, I switched gears. "Listen, you're just here to let Victor's father know how much you guys like Victor and want him to come back to the team, okay?" Trevor nodded his head.

I knocked on the door and someone yelled something in Russian from inside. I knocked again and said, "Hello?"

"Come in!" I heard, this time in English.

We opened the door and what we saw was against at least a few dozen laws I'm sure. There was a dentist's chair in the living room, with a patient in it, and there was Victor's father putting some fillings in and there was Victor helping out as his assistant. I'm not sure you heard me, I said the man had his dentist office in his living room, two feet away from the kitchen trash.

"Come in, come in. I'm almost done," Victor's father said.

The place was no bigger than mine and two people were sitting in the "waiting room," meaning the couch behind the dentist chair. Two cats were running around the apartment. Trevor watched in horror as Victor's dad leaned into the drill he had placed in the patient's mouth. "Okay, rinse." And he gave him vodka to clean his mouth with. If I'm lyin' I'm dyin'.

Victor's father told the people who were waiting to give him five minutes and we stepped into the hallway to talk for a second.

I started. "I know you need Victor here to help and I totally respect that but is there any way we can have him one day a week for the games? He doesn't even have to come to practice anymore.

Victor's father thought for a second. "How much?"

"What?"

"How much for him to play?"

"Wait...you want me to pay you so Victor can play on the team?"

"Exactly. How much?"

"I can't pay you any money."

"Then he doesn't play. I need him here for business," he said. "He plays baseball for what? He makes money here. He works and then he goes to college. Baseball doesn't pay for college."

"It could," I said as I noticed for the first time that neither Victor nor his father was wearing plastic gloves. "People get baseball scholarships all of the time."

"Scholarship?"

We talked for a few more minutes but I had to get out of there before I saw him work on another patient. I'm scared enough of the dentist. Just the thought of this bare-handed Russian drilling people's mouths while pouring shots of vodka freaked me the fuck out.

The next game came and nobody had heard from Victor. It was about fifteen minutes from game time when Simon walked up to me and said, "No Victor, huh?"

"Nope."

"You want me to fake a seizure?" he said.

"Fake a seizure?"

"Yeah," he said like he couldn't believe I was even questioning it. "I do it all of the time when I go to restaurants and don't want to pay the bill."

"Wait. First of all, you're twelve. What restaurants are you going to?"

"Coach, don't worry about what restaurants I go to."

I couldn't believe I was even having this conversation, and before I could ask my next question, I looked up and saw Victor and his father walking to the field. The whole team ran out and patted Victor on the head. His father walked up to me and said, "We are here."

"Thanks for coming."

"Yes. I want to hear more about this scholarship later. Sounds good. I like." And he walked to the stands. I probably should have told him right then and there that he misunderstood what I was saying but, eh, what was the big deal? Maybe he was going to get a scholarship. (Side note:

he didn't get a scholarship and is now an eighteen-year-old dentist, who works out of his father's living room.)

We won that day. This team of misfits, this team of nonathletes, this little United Nations of a team was going to the playoffs, and with Victor on the mound, we had a chance against anyone. Even the Mexicans.

We won our first playoff game and since the league was so small if you won one game you were in the championships.

When the championship game rolled around the following weekend the park was packed. I was trying really hard not to take it too seriously but I'd be lying to you if I told you I wasn't. The fact that this team made it this far was amazing and to have another opportunity to play the team that beat us 27-0 showed just how far we had come. I wanted to beat them so badly. I just had to remember that I wasn't playing in the game.

We really had a chance to slay Goliath. The game was tied 1-1 after the fourth inning and you could see the other team starting to crack a little. The coach, who had been so calm and happy at our first game, was starting to lay into his team a little. I think they had beaten everybody in our league by at least twenty runs, so to be tied with two innings to go had made him a bit nervous.

In the top of the sixth inning, the other team scored three runs. I sat everyone down on the bench and said,

"Guys, this is our last at-bat but no matter what happens, we won this game. I don't care if we score ten runs or none, when this game ends, we are all winners."

Barf. Are you kidding me? I didn't fuckin' say that shit.

I said, "I don't mean to sound surprised but can you believe we have a chance to win this game? Those guys are the best Little League team I've ever seen and all we have to do is luck out, score a few, and we win."

The kids looked around at each other and Simon said, "You really need to work on your pep talks, coach." He was right. It was pretty awful.

There were two outs and nobody on when Poison Ivy came up to the plate. The good news was he was fast as shit. The bad news was he hadn't touched a ball all year long. His first swing was the single ugliest thing I had ever seen on a baseball field. It looked like he had been attacked by a swarm of bees and he was trying to fight them off with his bat. The second pitch was a slow curveball that he swung at so far in advance his bat actually hit the ball on the back swing and it rolled into fair territory.

Run!

I don't think anyone, including the umpire, had ever seen anything like that before, so everyone just stood still for a second.

Run!

Poison Ivy took off and by the time the pitcher got to the

ball it was way too late. We had a runner on first base and we still had ourselves a ballgame.

Rodrigo was up next. A smart man would tell you that in this situation there's no way you should try to steal second base. Luckily, nobody ever accused me of being a smart man. Fuck it.

Of course, if Poison Ivy got thrown out, I would have been severely beaten by the Russian track suit mafia but that black Russian was really fast and he slid in safe.

On the second pitch he saw, Rodrigo hit a single up the middle and Ivy scored easily from second. We were down by two and Trevor was up next. I'm not sure I can tell you how nervous I was. After all, it hadn't been his idea to play; it had been mine, and my thinking was that he would come away with a lot of memories. Well, if he got out there and we ended up losing in a heartbreaker, he'd have a memory all right. It would be a memory that sucked ass. Trevor walked up to the plate and I could hear my heart beating in my neck.

Trevor always wore his helmet way down over his eyes so that he had to crane his neck up to see the pitcher. He looked down at me and I clapped my hands. "It's all good, T. Give it a ride." Which was code for "Please hit this fucking ball so I don't feel like even more of an asshole for making you play."

What I was hoping for was something that Trevor would

remember for the rest of his life. Realistically, I didn't care if he got hit by a pitch. I just wanted him to get on base and not feel bad about himself.

"Time out!" I said. I walked halfway down the baseline to talk to Trevor. When I got closer I could see his hands trembling.

"Just thought you should know that I sharted a little in the third inning," I said.

"What?" he asked, almost like he was being brought out of a trance.

"I thought I was going to fart and I pooped just a little."

"Why did you do that?"

"I didn't do it on purpose. It just happened."

"That's gross," he said.

"Tell me about it. I keep thinking someone stepped in poop and then I remember that it's in my pants."

He smiled.

"Just thought you should know." I started to walk away. "You wanna go for ice cream after the game?" I asked.

"Sure," he said and he walked back to the plate.

I know, I know, I really have to work on my pep talks. He stepped back in the box, lifted his helmet up out of his eyes, and dug in. The pitcher reared back, threw a pitch, and Trevor hit a rocket into the outfield! Holy shit. Because we were at a shitty little park, we played at a field with no fences and the ball seemed to roll forever.

"Run, T, run!"

He might be the hero. Did I luck into being father of the year?

Crushed. As Trevor rounded second, their center fielder was just getting to the ball.

Shit. This was going to be really close.

If it had been anyone else running the bases, I would have sent him home without a second thought. But I didn't want Trevor to get thrown out at the plate to end the game and have it be me who sent him. I wanted him to love baseball. There was no way I could send him. I was putting my hand up to hold him when I looked at his face.

He was smiling.

As he was running the bases to potentially score the tying run he was fucking smiling.

I had to send him.

"Go, T! Go!" I screamed as I waved him around third base.

At the same time, the shortstop caught the ball in left field and threw it home. Man, Trevor was hauling ass. It was going to take a perfect throw to get him. As he slid into home, there was no doubt in my mind that he was going to be safe. There was no way it wouldn't happen. This was destiny. As a fan of sports movies, to get a chance to live a real-life *Rudy* or *Bad News Bears* was insane. I know it was just kids playing baseball but the season had turned into so much more than that for everyone. As the catcher applied the tag, I knew I had made the right decision in making Trevor play. This truly was a memory he would take with him forever.

"He's out!" the umpire yelled.

Maybe I was wrong.

The other team poured out of their dugout and formed a dog pile at home plate. I watched Trevor walk away from the pile and back to the dugout with his head down. This was going to come out in therapy in a few years for sure.

As the bench cleared and I shook hands with all of the parents and thanked them for their time and support, I looked over to see Trevor sitting on home plate with his head in his hands. I walked over to him and put my hand on his shoulder. I knew that I needed to apologize to him for making him play and for sending him to home. I had to take away his pain if I could.

I knelt down next to him and said, "I'm really sorry, T."

He lifted his head up and said, "For what? That was awesome."

I couldn't believe it.

"Now I know why you like baseball so much."

Holy shit, if that had been me on the field, I would have ripped my jersey off and cried until there was no fluid left in my body. He and I were going to have a beautiful base-ball future together.

We didn't.

It turned out that what he loved was the competition. Not so much baseball. Guess what sport he did like though? Yup, soccer. And he was good. Really good. I don't know if it was karma but the universe definitely got the last laugh on this one.

If only I hadn't sent him home.

CHAPTER 7

Halloween

I love Halloween.

Love, love, love, love, love. And not just because all of the women's costumes make them look like sluts. That's a bonus that came as I got older. I've always loved Halloween. It was always my favorite holiday and I'm not sure there's really a close second. I know a lot of people like Christmas or Hanukkah (I'm a Jew and I'm still confused about how to spell that word) and I can't argue with that. Presents are pretty damn cool but, holy shit, there's a whole lotta family time happening over those few weeks. Some would say too much family time. Family time that always seems to lead to tears, drinking, and sometimes the emergency room. Halloween doesn't have any of those problems.

Some people really like New Year's Eve and to those people I would say, "You're stupid." Every year people get these grand plans in their heads and every year these people run into a shitload of traffic and go to parties that are gigantic letdowns. I call New Year's Eve "amateur night" because that's when people who don't go out all year head to the bars and get shitfaced like a bunch of amateurs. And the accessories? Fights, puking, glow sticks... the worst. That's why you can throw St. Patrick's Day into the same category. I guess birthdays are pretty cool, but for a lot of us, they're just reminders that we're closer to fifty than twenty and that kinda sucks.

But Halloween is the best. Now and when I was a kid.

I will say the Halloween experience back then was way different than it is now. To begin with, we didn't have Party City or anywhere like that to get costumes. My mom made mine. She would go into the attic, open up this dusty-ass trunk, and pull out some of my brothers' old clothes.

"Let's see what you're going to be this year."

All my friends got their costumes made by their moms. I had one friend who was a ghost every year. His mom was lazy as fuck. There was one year when my mom made me a flower. A homemade flower. Not great. Especially since she used glue to make the petals stick to my face. While we were trick-or-treating, my friends thought it would be funny to play "She loves me, she loves me not" and they started ripping the petals off of my face one by one. When they were done, I looked like I had round, red birthmarks that went around my face.

When I was a kid, we didn't have to trick-or-treat with our parents. *Huge* difference. Not only did we not want them there but they didn't want to go with us either. I can't decide if this generation of kids is spoiled or if our parents just didn't give a shit what happened to us. I had to take my son and some of his friends trick-or-treating one year because they weren't allowed to go by themselves, and I have to say, it was one of the most disappointing evenings of my entire life. They just didn't understand how amazing Halloween is. Free candy? What's better than that? Well, in today's age of iPhones and Xboxes, apparently a lot of things. These kids sucked. They had no energy, no nothin'. First off, they showed up at my door with costumes all crooked and some masks resting on top of their heads, and they were all holding these pansy-ass little plastic pumpkins. Not a great start.

"We're ready to go trick-or-treating," they said all lackluster.

No, you're not. Go home and get your freakin' pillowcases right now. That's when you'll be ready! A tiny plastic pumpkin? Are you kidding me? When I was a kid, we grabbed our pillowcases and slung them over our shoulders and walked down the street like someone who just robbed a house. We were pirates with our booty. We didn't skip down the street with a plastic orange pumpkin. We would have gotten our asses beat.

I made all of the kids get their costumes on straight and told them that I better hear them say "Trick or treat" from the sidewalk or they wouldn't get that candy. I know, I know. You're saying, "They're just kids. Relax." Uh...go fuck yourself. It's Halloween! Get excited! You're getting free shit so the least you can do is say trick or treat and say it with feeling.

We went to our first house and the kids all said, "Trick or treat" nice and loud. The woman smiled, put something in their pathetic pumpkins, and closed the door. They walked back to the sidewalk and I said, "Let's see whatcha got."

I looked in the pansy-ass pumpkin and saw an apple. No, she did not. An apple? I eyed the kids and said, "You guys know what to do with that apple, right?"

"Eat it?" my son said.

Huh?

"Get over here. Get over here!" I called to the group. "You take the apple out of that feeble little pumpkin and you throw it at that house right now. What is wrong with you kids? Break a window. Have some respect for Halloween."

"But, Daddy, they're nutritious and delicious."

Nutritious and delicious? I ate so much candy on Halloween I shit a Zagnut bar. I had diabetes by November first. I was no quitter. These kids had no concept of the fun you're supposed to have on this night. You're supposed to cause trouble. You're supposed to wrap toilet paper around a tree. You're supposed to scare somebody. It's Halloween! That's why I liked it so much—because you were almost given the okay to stir shit up.

But these kids from their sterile, dull generation were getting bored fast. After only half an hour, mind you, I had one kid tell me, "I'm tired. I'm ready to go home." Tired? Do you ever remember being tired on Halloween? Of course not! You ran home, dumped out your pillowcase, maybe snorted a Pixy Stix, and ran out the door. Maybe you ran right back in to tell your father, "Don't you eat my Snickers, old man. I swear if you eat my Snickers this year I'm gonna be so mad! Eat the Rolos! You can eat the Rolos!" And then you ran back out. We literally trick-or-treated until people in houses turned their lights off. That was the sign that they were done.

Another of the kids actually told me, "I'm ready to go. I've got enough candy." Enough candy? How is that possible? You're nine. You saying you've got enough candy is like me saying I've seen enough boobs. Never gonna happen. At nine, candy is your boobs and tonight you get free candy. Shop till you drop! If someone told me that once a year I could dress up and every door I knocked on someone would show me their boobs, I would still be trick-or-treating. I would have never gone back home. You'd see me crawling around neighborhoods, muttering, "One more house. I know I can make it to one more house."

We also used to get as much candy as we could because at the end of the night we counted pieces and you always wanted to be the person with the most candy. I couldn't believe they didn't do that anymore. When I told Jacob about getting the most candy he said, "Why did you do that? Did you win something?'

No.

"Did you get your name in the paper or something?"

No.

"Did grandma and grandpa care?"

No.

"Well, that sounds stupid."

You're stupid. You and your pumpkin-carrying friends are all stupid. How about that? They didn't throw apples, they didn't want to stay out all night, they didn't count candy...I couldn't believe what I was seeing. The complete and total collapse of Americana. And then, when I didn't think it could get any worse, it did. We walked up to a house with a bowl of candy on the patio and in that bowl was a note that read, "Please take one."

When I was growing up that meant...one...whole...

bowl. We took everything, bowl included. Sorry if you were stupid enough to leave your stuff on the patio; you'll find it in the bushes down the street. When I saw the bowl I thought, "Finally. Their animal instincts will kick in here. Years of Halloween genetics surely haven't been totally lost on these pussies, have they? I mean, it's a free bowl of candy, somebody's gonna grab it, right?"

Nope.

I walked up and they were picking through it trying to find their favorite piece of candy. Piece. As in, one piece. Imagine a wolf walking up to his cubs and seeing them eating an organic green salad with goat cheese. That's what it was like for me. They had just about broken my Halloween spirit. I walked in a daze for the next fifteen minutes. What was the point of this exactly? They didn't care how much candy they got. All they wanted to do since the minute we left the house was go home and play Xbox. They couldn't have given a shit about Halloween or anything that came with it.

It was time to call it a night.

As I walked up to the group, I saw my son looking across the street at some older kids who weren't in costume but who were all carrying pillowcases. They had just jumped out of the bushes to scare a group of younger kids and were laughing about it. I recognized that crew. That's the next stage. The stage where you still want candy but most people think you're too old to knock on doors to get it. So what do you do? You take it from the small and the weak. When I was growing up there was always a group of kids who egged cars, toilet papered houses, and took candy from little trick-or-treaters. I remember seeing those guys and thinking, "That looks awesome."

And one Halloween, when I was sixteen, I decided it was my turn.

Two of my buddies (Kevin and Jimmy) and I decided to head out on Halloween to cause a little bit of trouble. We had a plan in place and it was going to be the best Halloween ever. I had two responsibilities: booze and transportation. My parents had a good amount of liquor in the house and they hardly ever drank, so every week-end I would steal a bunch of it and head out. When I say "steal," I don't mean I took a whole bottle and walked out the door. I siphoned a little out of each bottle and made a witches brew of liquor in one of my mother's empty ma-son jars.

Part vodka, part rum, part tequila, part gin, part whiskey, part scotch, part bourbon, part vermouth, part crème de menthe, and part Campari all topped off with or-ange juice. Man, I thought I was cool walking out of the house with that ass mixture. Just writing it all down makes me realize why every girl I ever went out with in high school ended up puking.

Transportation was a breeze because my parents, for the first time in forever, had just bought a second car. I know to some of you that doesn't sound like a big deal but we didn't have any money when I was growing up, so a second car was huge.

It was a gray, four on the floor, Reliant K station wagon.

You can just bet that all the ladies were dying to get in on a little of that action. It actually turned out to be a pretty damn useful car. We carried kegs in it, there was plenty of room in the back for some dry humping, and, best of all, that fuckin' station wagon laid the best rubber out of any car I have ever driven. I mean it left some serious tracks. You think someone looks like a douchebag laying rubber in a sports car? Well, you ain't seen nothin' until you see a station wagon do it.

Douchebag + Pathetic = Me in High School.

I went to pick up Kevin first. His parents were the parents who were completely fooled by their kid. You ever know people like that? Their kid is a complete fuckup, lies all of the time, grades are horrible, always getting in trouble but the parents still believe every word he says. That was Kevin and his folks.

"I'll see you guys later," Kevin said.

"What time?" his father said.

"No later than eleven. You know me, Dad. I don't like being out too late."

"I know you don't. Josh, make sure you don't keep him out too late this time," his father said.

I couldn't believe what he got away with. Either his parents were really that stupid and they believed it was my fault every time he didn't come home and there was puke in their bushes, or they couldn't wait to get him out of the house so they could have sex. That is a possibility, by the way. For those of you who don't know, your parents have sent you out of the house so they could have sex. I guarantee it. Especially when you got older.

After I assured Kevin's father that I would have him home early, Kevin and I got into my car and took off to get Jimmy.

"What do you think of this?" Kevin said and he proceeded to take out the biggest joint I had ever seen in my entire life.

"Holy shit," I said. "Where did you get that?"

"Stole it from my dad. You got your mason jar full of ass?"

"Yup."

Our basic plan was to be assholes. We really hadn't thought it out too much further than that. Jimmy had brought eggs, tomatoes, and stink bombs; Kevin had brought balloons to fill with water; and I had brought the greatest getaway car ever. It was going to be a good night.

When I was that age, I thought being a douche on Halloween was a rite of passage. Like being bar mitzvahed, only completely different. Unfortunately for me and my friends, the fates must have heard what we were planning on doing because it came back to us tenfold.

We thought the eggs would be a fun place to start the evening so we headed out to a neighborhood where we were sure there would be a lot of people walking around. Our one rule was no youngsters. The only people we were fucking with had to be at least thirteen years old. Kevin and Jimmy started drinking from the mason jar and we were off. I should have known right away that it was going to be a bad night because on our way to start egging, a car cut me off. Not a big deal really, but I did lay on the horn to let him know that I didn't appreciate it and just kept driving. About thirty seconds after I honked the horn, the horn beeped again, only this time I hadn't touched it.

BEEP-BEEP.

What the—? I drove for about a minute and…*BEEP-BEEP.* Son of a bitch. My horn was going off for no reason and it did so intermittently for the whole night. There was talk of bailing on the whole plan because if my horn blew when we were trying to surprise people it would really screw things up. Kevin took a long gulp from the mason jar and said, "They'll never know what hit 'em." That was just the right amount of cheesy and stupid for three testosterone-filled idiots to scream at the top of their lungs and drive on into the night.

The reason this neighborhood was so good for what we were planning was that it was huge, with so many streets and backstreets. There was no way anyone would be able to follow us even if they wanted to. As we pulled in, we immediately saw our first targets walking down the street: four teenage boys who were sticking things in people's mailboxes. Perfect. I had no problem with being an asshole to assholes. As we drove toward them, Kevin and Jimmy got an egg in each hand and rolled down the windows. I slowed down the car a little and just as we were about two hundred yards away...

BEEP-BEEP.

No fucking way.

The kids turned around and saw Jimmy and Kevin hanging out the windows with eggs and they started throwing whatever they were putting in the mailboxes at my car.

Splash! Splash! Splash!

They hit the car.

Kevin and Jimmy pulled their heads back in the windows and we sped away. I turned on my wipers to clear the windshield and said, "That fucking horn! Can you believe that?"

I turned to the backseat and saw Jimmy was drenched

with water. "Damn, dude, they killed you with water balloons."

Jimmy stared intently back at me. "That's not water."

"It seriously smells like piss back here," Kevin said.

Pee bombs? We got doused with pee bombs? Right out of the gate? This was not good.

Jimmy sat there frozen like a mummy for a few minutes, and then he said, "What the hell am I supposed to do now? I'm covered in urine."

Let me tell you something. I guarantee you I never in my life thought I would hear one of my best friends say that to me from the backseat of my car. Never. I didn't know whether to laugh or pull over and give the guy a hug. Being a teenager with no moral compass or sense of decency, I laughed. We did pull over about a quarter mile up so Kevin could disconnect the horn and Jimmy could take a leak. Ah, irony.

There was no getting around the fact that the car was going to smell like a toilet if we didn't roll down the windows. But it was October in New England and too cold to drive around with the windows down the whole time. So we alternated. When we couldn't stand the smell anymore we rolled down the windows, and when it got too cold we rolled them back up. Another unfortunate victim in the pee drenching was the eggs. When Kevin and Jimmy fell back into the car, they had dropped all but one of their eggs and Kevin accidentally crushed the rest of the eggs that were in a bag on the seat.

One egg left in a stinky-pee car.

The plan was to circle around, find those kids and this time get them with tomatoes. Our confidence as badasses had been stripped a little bit, but one good tomato bombing would put us right back on track to being assholes for the rest of the night. Jimmy was chugging my mason jar concoction, doing anything he could to get the taste of piss out of his mouth, and Kevin had just lit up his Bob Marley–sized joint.

For those of you who don't know, back then joints had to be Bob Marley–sized because the weed was so weak. You could literally smoke a joint by yourself and all you would get was a headache. These days, with all of the medicinal weed out there, if you smoke a whole joint by yourself you'll be couch-locked for hours. I made the mistake once of eating too much of a "medicated" blueberry muffin and let me tell you it was not pretty. I thought my TV was interactive. Probably don't need to say much more than that and I really hope my kids skipped this paragraph.

We circled around three times and couldn't find the group anywhere so we decided to start in on the stink bombs. The stink bombs were what I was looking forward to the most. A stink bomb up close can definitely ruin a day. I was in a friend's car once when someone slipped one in an open back window and it stunk up his car for weeks.

We drove down the street looking for the perfect victims when we came upon a guy and a girl who were making out on someone's lawn. He was lying on top of her so we figured if we parked the car a hundred yards away, one of us could run up, put the stink bomb in his costume, and run away.

Genius.

In the car, this seemed like the best idea in the entire world. Kevin volunteered to go do it because Jimmy had really caught the brunt of our ill-prepared last plan. But Jimmy wasn't having it.

"This one's mine," he said drunkenly as he got out of the car.

Kevin and I watched him stumble down the street toward our two victims and I said, "This might be the best trick ever."

"Yup."

Jimmy disappeared around the corner. Before I could say another word, he came sprinting back screaming something.

"What's he saying?" I asked.

"No idea," Kevin said as he rolled down the window.

"Start the car! Start the fucking car!" Jimmy screamed. And behind him, we saw this mountain of a person chasing him.

Uh-oh.

I started the car, Kevin opened the back door, and as Jimmy got closer we could see a dark smudge of something covering his left cheek. Luckily for us, and Jimmy in particular, this big guy was not fast, and Jimmy jumped in the car and we sped away. We had driven for about two seconds when Kevin and I noticed a new foul smell in the car.

"What the fuck is that?" I asked.

It was Jimmy.

"Fuck! Fuck, fuck, fuck, fuck fuck!" he yelled.

He told us he had the stink bomb in his hand ready to lay it down, but when he turned the corner only the girl was on the lawn. He looked to his right and the guy, who had just finished taking a leak in the bushes, was standing next to him. Jimmy said he tried to distract the guy by trying to throw the stink bomb at him but the guy stopped his hand, took the stink bomb from him, and smeared it across his face. Jimmy squirmed away, ran back to the car, and the rest was history.

Poor Jimmy. He literally smelled like he had crawled out of a Porta Potty.

It was time to go home. The night of being douchebags had ended in complete failure. We drove through the neighborhood in silence until Jimmy started tossing the tomatoes out the window like a madman. "This is the worst Halloween ever! I drank piss, I have a shit smell under my nose, and I don't have any candy!" Just as he threw the last tomato out the window, we spotted the group of kids who made it rain urine on my car.

Noooooooooooooooooooooooooo!

We had nothing left to throw and we could see they were loaded up with balloons in their hands. I tried to speed past them but...

Splash! Splash! Splash!

It was too late.

We were clearly not good at this.

Jimmy finished the rest of the mason jar and Kevin was halfway through his joint when I heard Jimmy slur, "Pull over."

I pulled to the side of the road, Jimmy opened the door, and I heard him say, "I'm at least getting some fucking candy." Whatever that meant.

Kevin, who was sitting in front with me because Jimmy smelled so bad, said, "I cannot wait to tell people about this at school on Monday."

"Are you kidding me? I'm already trying to come up with a nickname for him." We both laughed and then we heard yelling from outside the car.

"Stop it! Give me my candy back!"

I looked behind me and drunk-ass Jimmy was walking back to the car, holding a pillowcase that still had a kid attached to it.

I got out of the car. "Jimmy, give him his candy back and let's go. Not kidding. Give him the candy or I leave you here."

As drunk as he was, Jimmy knew what he was doing was wrong. And just as he was about to let go, the kid said, "Yeah, shit stain. Give me my candy!"

Shit stain. I liked that nickname. I liked it a lot.

Jimmy did not.

He wrestled the pillowcase out of the kid's hands, took two steps toward the car and... *Wham!* He got smacked in the side of the face with a Wiffle ball bat.

The kid's friend who was trick-or-treating with him and who was dressed as a baseball player, screamed, "Give him his candy back, asshole!"

Jimmy fucking snapped. He started screaming and throwing candy in the car and tearing at his shirt like he was trying to rip his own clothes off to get to his heart. Seeing a crazed Jimmy, the kids freaked out and ran as fast as their little legs could take them into the night. Kevin got out of the car, took one look at Jimmy and the huge red welt on the side of Jimmy's face, and started laughing the laugh of a guy who had smoked a gigantic joint by himself. It was insane. I finally talked Jimmy back into the car, drove him and Kevin home, and thanked my lucky stars when I pulled into my driveway.

Monday at school was amazing.

I'm a guy who thoroughly enjoys when things like that happen. The perfect storm of awful does not occur too often, so when it does, if you're lucky enough to be there it truly is a blessing. Shit Stain came to school with a huge red mark that covered his right cheek, and Kevin and I told as many people as we could about what had happened. It really was close to a perfect day until about one o'clock. I was sitting in my English class when the principal and two uniformed policemen entered our class. The kid who sat behind me was always in trouble so I moved over a little, waiting for him to walk past me, when I heard, "Mr. Wolf, can you come with us please?"

What the fuck?

When I got to the principal's office, Kevin and Shit Stain were already there. What could this possibly be about? It couldn't be about Halloween because as far as I knew there was no law against getting your ass handed to you for an entire night. The cops looked incredibly serious as our principal sat behind her desk.

"Where were you guys on Halloween?" she asked.

"Driving around," I responded.

"And you did what?" she said.

"Nothing really. Just drove around," I said.

One of the police officers looked so mad, it was like he had to stop himself from punching a hole in my chest and shitting in it. "Bullshit!" he told us. "We know you three assholes were out stealing candy from little kids. Isn't that right?"

Uh-oh. How did he know that? The one detail we left out of our story at school was the part where Jimmy terrorized those kids. As funny as it was that he got clocked with the bat, even we weren't down with him stealing that candy.

"I have no idea what you're talking about. We didn't do anything like that."

"Really?" he said. "That's weird because the kid who you scumbags pulled a knife on"—what?—"described your car and wrote down your license plate as you were driving off."

What?

"So, do you want to stick with that story or should we start dealing with the truth?"

The knife was a nice touch added by the kid, one I can't say I wouldn't have done myself. But holy shit. With the way that night went, it figured that the kid Jimmy had tried to grab some candy from was Dick Tracy Jr. Wrote down my license plate? The kid clearly watched way too much TV.

This was not something we were going to be able to get out of. Besides the license plate evidence, we had walked around school all day talking about what dirt bags we had been that night. There was no getting out of it. We just had to convince the police somehow that nobody had used a knife. Ultimately, the huge red mark that the Wiffle ball bat had left helped convince them. They thought it was a little weird that a tiny kid would attack three teenagers who were holding knives with a Wiffle ball bat.

So when my son saw those kids across the street, I wondered how he would respond. He had just seen them scare a group of kids and saw them hide in the bushes waiting for the next group to pass. I thought I got my answer when he turned his back to them and started talking with his friends but then he turned around, holding an apple, and threw it at the kids in the bushes. And just like a pro, as soon as he let go of it, he looked down, pretending not to be involved.

Not me. I watched that bad boy make it all the way across the street and land right on top of one of the kids' head.

"Who threw that? Who threw that?" the kid yelled.

When nobody answered, the older kids walked away and as soon as they did, my son and his group started laughing and high-fiving. They got it! It finally sank in! That's Halloween! I walked over to them and said, "Who's ready to go to the house with the full-size candy bars?"

As we walked over there, I was a little ashamed of myself. I hadn't planned on taking them to this house because I didn't feel they deserved it. I had given up on these little pussies and I shouldn't have. Yes, everyone grows up differently but there's a little hooligan in everyone. You just have to know how to pull it out.

And now we were on the hunt for the full-size candy bar, which was the best find when you were out there going door to door. It was like an endangered species. You had to be smart to track it down.

The guy who handed them out was an older man who loved when kids came to the door, but he creeped them out because he looked like he had died in 1986. What was really the important thing about him was that he didn't know Halloween etiquette. He never turned on his front porch light. No porch light, no trick-or-treaters. No trick-or-treaters, lots of candy left. His house was a gold mine that only a few of us knew about, and my son and his friends had just earned themselves a trip.

The kids were getting antsy. They wanted to know where this secret house was, and as soon as they started talking about it, there it was. It was a tiny house tucked behind a bigger one on the same lot. They had two different owners but most people looked at the small house in the back and assumed it was the pool house or guesthouse. As we stood in front of the property, we saw another group of kids walking down the street.

One of Jacob's friends started to call out to them. "Hey guys! We're about to get—"

I plastered my hand over his mouth. *Shh.* You don't

tell the enemy anything and that's exactly what that other group was: the enemy. It's every team for themselves and we were the team that was going in for the full-size.

I watched the kids walk around the front house and disappear into the back. I didn't walk to the door with them. I figured I might as well give them as much freedom as I was allowed to. Plus, truth be told, I had a couple of flasks on me and I needed them out of sight so I could drink.

A little while later the kids came running back more excited than I had seen them all night. "Dad! Look! Look what we got!" Jacob said.

I looked down and they all had the jumbo Twix package. Jackpot.

"Great job, guys! Great job!"

As we walked down the street, the kids told me how old the guy was, how he said we were just the second group to come to his door, and how he could barely see what everyone's costumes were. They could not stop talking about how cool the dark little house was and how nobody else knew where it was except them and that they're going to go to that house every year from now on. Halloween was in their bones. It was awesome but the lesson was just beginning.

When we got to the top of the street, I gathered them in a group and said, "I know that the full-size is amazing, right?"

"Right!"

"And I think we've worked hard tonight and we deserve another, right?"

"Right!"

"Here's what we're gonna do. You guys switch your costumes around and we'll go back for another round. He'll never know and you guys will get another Twix. Am I right?"

This was their moment. This was their time to show me what they had learned. This was their time to accept the baton that I was handing to them.

"But, Dad, that's cheating."

Apparently I had overestimated these kids.

First of all, it was not cheating; it was trying. Going for two full-size candy bars from the same house was a big-time move! If you could successfully pull the old costume switch, you could go down in Halloween lore. I thought these kids had turned the corner and were ready for the big leagues, but apparently I was dead wrong.

I tried everything. I even told them that if we didn't go back the old guy might be stuck with a bunch of candy that he'll have to eat and at his age that could kill him. It was our moral duty to go back to that house one more time.

Nothing. They thought that it was wrong. "Don't you know that?" one of the kids asked. "You're a grownup."

It was clear these kids didn't understand fun and tradition and I was done trying to show them. We all started walking back to my house and, frankly, I couldn't wait to get there. My second flask was running low and alcohol was the only thing making the evening even remotely tolerable. I couldn't believe that one of the cornerstones of my childhood was going to die with this generation.

About a block from my house, the kids all decided they wanted to hit one more house. At that point, I really didn't give a shit what they did as long as we were making our way to my place. They all ran up to the house and on the porch was a skeleton holding a bowl. That bowl had a note in it and that note read, "Please take one." I heard them talking about what piece they each wanted to take and how they needed to leave enough candy for the next group. And I snapped.

I walked up to the porch, took one of the kids' pumpkins, and said, "Give me that pansy-ass little pumpkin and let me show you how we do this old school."

I grabbed the bowl and started to pour the candy into the pansy-ass little pumpkin . . . when the skeleton grabbed my wrist! I heard someone scream like a bitch. That was the last straw. They didn't throw the apples, they were tired, they wanted to go home early, they wouldn't do the costume switch and now, now they're letting out high-pitched shrieks? I had had enough. I turned to the kids and said, "Hey, who's screaming like a girl?"

My son pointed at me. "You."

I said, "No, I didn't."

The guy dressed like the skeleton took off his mask and, laughing, he said, "Yeah, you did, bro! I grabbed your wrist and you screamed like this...Aaaahhhhh! Jazz hands and everything!" He shook his hands in the air.

I couldn't believe it. I screamed like a bitch in front of kids I had been calling soft all night. None of them screamed; they all thought it was awesome. But me, Mr. Tough Guy, Mr. My-Generation-was-the-best-you-kids-get-off-of-my-lawn, let out a guttural, instinctual lady-like shrill. Maybe they were a little tougher than I thought. Just because my generation was okay with taking shit that wasn't ours and throwing eggs at people didn't necessarily mean we knew how to have more fun or were more hard-core. Hell, when I was a kid, that skeleton would have sent me home crying. To be truthful, it almost did that night.

I turned to walk off the porch and the skeleton tapped me on the shoulder. I looked back at him and he handed me the plastic pumpkin that I had dropped.

"Get the kids some pillowcases. What is wrong with you?"

Some things never change.

P.S. When you have an infant, you can have sex right in front of them and they won't know what the hell is going on. The problem with that is you're having sex in front of your kid, which is pretty fucking disgusting. I'm not saying I've never done it; I'm just saying that it's disgusting.

As your kids get a little older, all it takes is a DVD and a snack and you've got a full hour and a half to sex it up as much as you want. Seriously, between the ages of three and seven, when you turn on that TV it's like the kids are in a trance. They don't hear or see anything that doesn't have to do with what's on that screen.

The problem comes when they're old enough to know what sex is and too old to dose up with Benadryl. That's when you have to send them out of the house. Why out of the house? Because they're old enough to know what the hell is going on in the bedroom with the door locked and the TV on full blast. And, most important, nobody should ever, ever, *ever* walk in on their parents having sex.

It's a scar that never goes away.

I didn't actually walk in on my parents having sex. But I did wake up early one morning and I walked past their room, with its door open, and they were having sex. Worst thing about it was that I made eye contact with my dad!

Yuck. I ran into the kitchen, shaking, drooling, and trying to scoop my fucking eyeballs out with a spoon. It was horrible!

My dad walked in fifteen minutes later like he was king of the world. He kinda milled around for a few seconds and then said, "Do you want me to make you some eggs?"

Eggs? Are you joking right now? I don't want you to touch a piece of food that I'm going to eat ever again.

CHAPTER 8

Stupidest Thing Ever

Have you ever done something so stupid that you're pretty sure there should be a new word to better describe how stupid you are?

I've never claimed to be the brightest person in the world. In fact, I would go so far as to say that I'm not even in the upper half of the IQ pool. If you base it on what I think is funny, I might have been riding the short bus to school. When the ketchup bottle makes a fart noise, I still laugh even if I'm by myself. I wake up in the morning and one of the first things I do after I get my coffee is look on YouTube for videos of people falling down. Hell, my favorite joke of all time is rubbing my nuts on other people's things and then watching them use it. I'm stupid. Not gonna argue that, but what I do have is common sense.

At least I thought I did.

When my ex and I first split up, my brother and I would spend nights shooting the shit and drinking in our apartment. I wasn't crushed by the split but I was scared shitless about how I was going to make everything work. I had nobody to ask, "Hey, when you're in your twenties, with no job or money and you have to take care of three kids, what should you do?" If your answer is drink, well, that was my answer, too.

Unfortunately, when that's your answer, you may at some point end up drunk in front of one of your kids. I remember the first time that happened. My brother and I had put a few back one night, and by a few I mean I was hammered.

My oldest, who had to be eight at the time, came stumbling out of the bedroom. "You guys are being so loud," he said.

"Sorry, buddy. Go back to sleep," I said. At least that's what I thought I said. When you're drunk and trying to pretend that you're not, the words that form in your head are never the ones that come out of your mouth. "Heeeeeeeeey, buddy! Did we wake you up? How about some ice cream?" was what came out instead.

"Are you drinking beer, Dad?"

Right or wrong, I had always made a point not to drink in front of my kids. So I tried to think of a good reason why I would be drinking. "I sure am. You know why?"

He shook his head.

"Because it makes you smarter." Ugh. I have a feeling that one is going to come back to haunt me.

Right then and there, my brother (who wasn't nearly as fucked up as I was) could have stepped in and said, "You know what, Trevor? Time to go back to sleep. We'll see you in the morning." Do you know why he didn't do that? Because he's an asshole just like me and keeping my son awake to talk to his drunk-ass father seemed like a much more interesting choice.

I have pictures from that night and they are the single most white-trash-looking pictures of my entire life. First of all, we were all shirtless. It was Los Angeles in the summer and air conditioning cost money so we used it sparingly. Second, in the pictures we were building a Pabst Blue Ribbon beer can pyramid on top of my—wait for it—wooden barrel dining room table. That's right. I had purchased a round dining room table that was made out of an old wooden barrel. I know it sounds bad but believe me when I tell you it was even worse. The worst thing about the table? Besides the fact that it was an old barrel that always smelled like SpaghettiOs and malt liquor? Besides the fact that it came with four matching wooden barrel chairs? Besides the fact that I was so poor I was keeping that piece of shit together with duct tape? The worst part about it was that the top of the table was only about two and a half feet off the ground. It was like a barrel table made for circus performers. The last thing that made those pictures the ultimate in white trash?

My son was drawing on me with a Sharpie.

Yup. My asshole brother, knowing how funny it would be later, told Trevor to get a Sharpie and start drawing. I told my brother I was pretty drunk and asked him if he thought it was a good idea. You know what he said?

"I think it's one of the best ideas ever."

Needless to say, those pictures are not in any family album.

Like I said, I've done a lot of stupid things in my life. As a matter of fact, I'm pretty sure I did only stupid things between the ages of sixteen and twenty-two. The absolute stupidest thing, bar none, happened in San Antonio, Texas, my freshman year in college. Let me just start by saying it was hot. Really hot. Like, sweaty-back, steering-wheel-too-hot-to-touch, nuts-stuck-to-the-side-of-your-leg, wanna-kill-someone kind of hot. It was the kind of hot where people don't go outside and on days like those, the San Antonio Zoo had started letting people in for free toward the end of the day. So, being broke-ass college students, my buddy Jock and I decided to head there.

After about an hour, the one thing I could say with complete certainty was that the San Antonio Zoo for sure has the largest collection of sleeping animals ever as- sembled. I know a lot of people say, "They're not coming out because it's so hot." Most of them are from Africa! I've never been to Africa but it looks pretty fucking hot in the movies. I think they're just bored out of their minds. For the lions and other predators, I bet being in a zoo is like being a guy in a strip club. You're just staring at things you want all day but you know, no mat- ter how hard you try and how many times they wipe glitter on you and say they love you, you'll never have them. Maybe that's why they don't ever move. They're depressed. Maybe the zoo needs to mix some Zoloft in with their raw meat.

The zoo was a ghost town and at one point a peacock walked in front of us, stopped, looked at us, and kept walk- ing. It was almost like he was saying, "What the hell are you two doing here?" Which wouldn't have been the first time an animal spoke to me. (I ate mushrooms one time with some friends and I swear a frog told me that "yogurt is very refreshing.") The zoo was going to be open for only fif- teen more minutes when we were passing by the rhino den. I've always been fascinated with rhinos. I mean, they've got a fucking horn on their face. Pretty damn cool. So I stopped to take a look as Jock went to look at the rhino's info.

"Lord," Jock said.

"What?" I asked.

"That's his name," Jock said. "The rhino's name is Lord."

We looked at Lord for a second.

"He is massive," I said.

"Can't believe he's just like a cow."

"What are you talking about?" I asked.

Jock went on to tell me how rhinos are just like cows in that "they're scared of people."

I couldn't believe what I was hearing. Hadn't he ever seen any of those safari videos where rhinos tip over tour buses? Although I shouldn't have been too surprised he hadn't seen those videos. After all, there was a big group of people my freshman year who had never seen a Jew, much less safari videos.

"Rhinos are vicious, Jock. Are you being serious right now?"

"They're pussies," he said.

"Okay, if they're such pussies, I'll give you $20 to get in the pen and another $20 to touch it on the ass."

There was no way in the world he would take that bet, I thought. Jump into a pen with a fucking rhino for twenty bucks? What kind of asshole does that? I'll tell you what kind of an asshole: my friend Jock.

"And you buy beer tonight," he demanded.

"Deal."

Let me set up what this pen looked like. It was about thirty feet long and twenty feet wide, with eight- to ten-foot rock walls and ground that was packed dirt. It was packed dirt because a thousand pound rhino had been walking on it. Lord was at the far end of the pen behind a tiny log wall that had an opening for him to get in and out of the pen through. I thought that if Jock got in that pen, there was no chance he was getting out. Jock was not a tall guy. And when I say he wasn't tall, I mean he's short—5'7" on a good day with cowboy boots and mousse in his hair. The walls were sheer rock and the only ladder out of there was down near Lord. If Jock got in, he would have to climb his way out, and I wasn't sure if Lord was into giving people a head start.

Jock was doing some stretching and I was egging him on, calling him a pussy and generally being the douchebag instigator that I am. I knew he was confident in his speed, because even though he was vertically challenged, he was the running back for our football team and fast as hell. Jock got to the wall, swung his legs over, and said, "I'm gonna drink a lot tonight, so you better bring your wallet."

Uh-huh. Gonna be extra hard to drink with a giant hole in your stomach.

I know some of you are probably thinking, "Josh, why would you let your friend do that? There's a good chance he could have died." Valid point. And one Jock and I have talked about many times. Truth is, I thought Jock would get to the side of the wall and then turn and tell me to go fuck myself. Maybe—and I mean *maybe*—he would jump in and then jump right back out. Maybe. I was convinced there was no way a human being would willingly get into a death box with a rhino. No way, no how, not a chance in the world. So when Jock actually disappeared from my sight I thought, "There's no way he just jumped into that rhino's pen." But he did. I looked over the side of the wall and there was Jock in the pen smiling at me.

"That's twenty you owe me already. Goin' to collect the other twenty right now."

No fucking way.

In shock, I watched Jock move toward Lord. "I'll give you your money, Jock. I'm not sure you should go any closer," I said.

"Like a cow," he said, referring to Lord.

I watched Jock walk toward Lord in his extra, extra tight cowboy jeans and cowboy boots. He was slipping on shit and dirt just walking. I thought, "If he has to run, he is fucked for sure." Every now and then, Jock would turn to me and start laughing. "Livin' the dream," he said a couple of times. Uh-huh.

I had been in Texas only a few months at that point and

had known Jock for less. If this had happened year four of my Texas experience I wouldn't have been surprised at all. Good ol' boys are a different kind of crazy and one I had never experienced, growing up in Massachusetts. I think rodeo is the best example I can give of that. Don't get me wrong, I had friends do crazy shit. I had a buddy of mine in high school steal a motorcycle and get chased by the cops for a good twenty minutes, only to hop off the bike and say, "I like the nightlife, baby." We stole stuff, drank at school, and did all of the normal high school things, but none of us, ever, *ever* stared at a bull and said, "Look at that thing. Fifteen hundred pounds of angry muscle that would like nothing better than to stomp a hole in my chest. I think I'm gonna get on top of it." That's a whole different level of crazy.

On top of that mentality, Jock had a few extra screws loose. A few years after this incident, Jock was at a bar when the TABC (Texas Alcoholic Beverage Commission) walked in and started checking people's IDs. Jock was twenty-one but the girl he was talking to was not. When the officer approached them, Jock looked him dead in the eye and said, "It's okay. She's with me." You see, Jock (after a few drinks) liked to tell people that he was with the CIA.

CIA.

That was his "go to."

Needless to say, that night didn't end too well for Jock and he was thrown in jail for the evening. He actually looked like he might get in a shitload of trouble so we had a friend of ours who was prelaw pretend to be his lawyer, go down to the sheriff's office wearing a suit that was a little too small, with a briefcase that had nothing in it, and had him start spewing whatever legalese he could pull out of his textbooks. I don't know if the sheriff didn't want to deal with the case of a drunk college kid or if he was so flabbergasted by what was sitting in front of him but he let Jock go with nothing but a slap on the wrist.

If I had known all of this, I might not have been so shocked when Jock jumped into the rhino's pen, but I might have tried harder to talk him out of it. The other reason I didn't try as hard as I could was, well, I wanted to see it. I certainly didn't want Jock to get hurt, and I told him I thought it was the worst idea of all time, but shit, if he was gonna do it, who was I not to watch? That would have just been rude.

As he slowly made his way across the pen, I looked around and saw nobody. I mean, nobody. No zoo workers. No people. Just me, Jock, and Lord. "This is how it always happens," I thought. It was like a scene in one of the thirty-seven *Final Destination* movies. Jock was about halfway to Lord and Lord hadn't noticed him yet. I couldn't believe it. Maybe he was right. Maybe rhinos really are like cows. Did I just get hustled?

And then it happened.

Jock was probably seven feet away from Lord when Lord made this...noise. Not sure exactly how to describe it because I had never heard anything like it before in my life, but let's just call it a "I'm going to stick my horn in your ass" noise because that's what it was. As soon as Lord made that noise, he turned and ran toward the opening in his gate and when that happened, Jock turned too.

I had never seen fear like that on someone's face before. It was a complete "holy shit, I was completely wrong and I'm about to die because of it" look, accompanied by an "I probably shouldn't be wearing cowboy boots right now because I'm running for my life" glance, with a touch of "I'm about to poop." And then he started running.

The race was on.

Man versus animal. Good versus evil. Life versus death. I seriously didn't know whether to laugh or cry. On the one hand, this was the ultimate in fear. I might watch my friend get impaled by a rhino. You couldn't think of much worse. On the other hand, I was watching someone get chased by a fucking rhino! How many people get to say that?

Jock was on a dead sprint back to the wall. I don't know if it was divine intervention or dumb luck but, even though he slipped fifteen times in his cowboy boots just walking in the pen, when he was running for his life, he didn't slip once. Good thing too because that rhino was really fucking fast. Faster than I could believe something that big with a suit of natural armor on could be. It was clear that Jock was going to beat Lord to the wall but then what? It wasn't a game of tag where the wall was "safe." He still had to get out of the pen. I leaned my body over the side of the wall as far as I could. Jock, at full speed, jumped and planted one foot in the middle of the rock wall. I reached over, grabbed his arm/shoulder/chest hair, and using his momentum swung him up over the wall and out of the pen.

I'm not sure if you know this or not but rhinos don't stop on a dime.

Bam! Lord and his horn ran into the wall half a second after Jock had been there.

Jock, having just come within a pube of death, lay on the ground, silent and exhausted. I, having just seen the funniest/craziest thing of all time, lay on the ground laughing my ass off. You know when you see someone take a really nasty digger on the ice or trip over something in the office and you wait a beat to laugh just to make sure they're not dead? That was this times one million. It took a little while for Jock to get his brain working again. After all, he had just been chased by a rhino. I imagine that would shake you up just a wee bit. After about five minutes of silence, Jock got up, dusted himself off, and headed toward the exit. We didn't say a word to each other until we got to the car and he looked at me and said, "Hippo, not rhino. Hippos are like cows."

Uh...that would be wrong, too.

When I say I did something stupid, it's not quite in the "run with rhinos" category but it was pretty damn dumb. I guess "stupid" falls into different slots. It depends on who you are. The crazy or stupid things that guys do are *way* different from the ones women do. Guys do a lot of crazy things that involve body noises and bodily fluids. Or just plain gross shit. I had a buddy of mine who would eat anything. I mean anything. I saw him put two cockroaches in a sandwich and eat it for six bucks.

On the other hand, women do things that guys would never, ever do. I got pulled over by a cop once with my girlfriend in the front seat and she was shitfaced. When the cop came up to my window, my girlfriend laughed and said, "Holy crap, you're ugly." I couldn't believe it.

"I'd keep her quiet if I were you," the officer said.

Yeah. That always works well with a drunk girl. Talk about her like she's not there and like you are in control of her. She'll love that.

"What did you say, Officer Ugly?" That's what she started calling him. "You think he can shut me up? He's not in charge of me and I can say whatever I want. I'm not breaking the law by calling you ugly. As a matter of fact, I think that's called stating a fact. And the fact is... you... are... *ugly*. There should be a law about how ugly you are. Tell him, Josh. Tell him how ugly he is. He can't do anything to you."

That was not true. He was actually carrying a nightstick and an entire belt full of other things that were designed to ruin my evening. He could do a lot to me.

As a guy, you grow up knowing that if you run your mouth someone will be there to shut it for you. Women don't have those consequences. They'll call bouncers "losers with no future" and walk away, leaving their dates there to take a punch to the face. They'll tell a group of huge dudes who are being loud to shut up and that all of the steroids they're doing are making their dicks small. Again, no consequence.

The stupid thing I did definitely came with consequences.

It was another night of drinking with my brother in my apartment and the conversation had turned to how much vagina he was seeing as opposed to how little I was getting. In an odd way, just knowing that at least someone was getting laid actually made me feel better. As he talked, I made the kids their lunches for the next day. I knew I wasn't going to be in any mood or shape to get up extra early in the morning so I figured I'd put together the lunches while at least one of my eyes was still open. (Just so you know, it's easy to tell when I'm drunk because my left eye blinks and my right eye never does. It's not even a little sexy.)

I woke up the next morning (it's probably more accurate to say I came to) with thirty minutes to get everyone ready and out the door. I actually had it down to a science at that point. Clothes were laid out, toast and banana were eaten for breakfast, teeth got brushed, and we were gone. I moved a little slower than usual that morning though because I felt like there were thirty little people with hammers trying to get out of my head and that my tongue had been sandblasted by goat feces.

Whenever I was hung-over, I told my kids it was "allergies." Man, do I miss the days when they believed everything I said. I had my youngest son convinced that not only did I know everything, but I was all-powerful. When we got my new car, he had no idea that I could control the radio from my steering wheel. He thought I could change the stations with my mind. It was awesome. He used to tell his friends how powerful I was and that they shouldn't ever think anything bad about me. I had a blast doing it until the father of one of the kids called me and said, "Would you please tell my son that you can control the radio from the steering wheel?"

"Of course. Put him on the phone."

The guy put his son on the phone and I said, "Do you think I control the radio with special powers?"

"Yes."

"Well, you're right. But don't tell your dad about them anymore or they'll make me blow up the planet. Understand?"

"Uh-huh."

So, hungover as hell, I grabbed my kids' lunches and herded them out the door. I dropped them all off at school, grabbed myself an Egg McMuffin (best hangover food ever), and went back to sleep. At about 11:00, I got a phone call from Jacob's school. Being Jewish, I sent Jacob to preschool at a temple (which we called the Jew School) because I wanted him to have some idea of where he came from. I also figured, knowing how non-religious I am, it was probably going to be the first and last real Jewish thing he ever did. Calling it the Jew School was actually funny until Jacob did it in front of the rabbi. Great man, but not so much with the sense of humor.

During that phone call I was asked to come to the school immediately. Jacob was okay but it was imperative that a school official talk to me right away.

Holy shit. What the hell could that be about?

I have to admit that I had gotten into a little trouble

at the school about three months earlier, though I'm not sure I would even call it "trouble." It was more that some of the parents weren't too pleased with how I went about my day-to-day. See, the school was only about ten minutes from my apartment but there were some days when I found myself near the school with about forty minutes to kill. Going home and sitting down for ten minutes only to have to get up and leave again was a pain in the ass, but staying in the Jew School parking lot was even worse, so I spent more than a few afternoons at the strip club near the school.

It was for convenience! Trust me, it wasn't for the daytime strippers. That was a different group of women altogether. One day I was in there and I actually heard one of the girls say, "Wait behind the curtain, baby. Mommy has to dance but I'll be right back." One day I walked in there and I saw one of the other fathers from the Jew School. I sat down next to him, and he said the same thing about being too early for pick-up and not wanting to wait in the parking lot. See? Not just me. After a few weeks, we had told a few other guys and they had told a few others, and I remember on one particular Tuesday there were about eight of us in there. A Tuesday! At noon! The manager started hooking me up with free dances because he thought I was the ringleader for this pack of over-the-hill perverts. He blocked sections

off for us, but he didn't really need to because we were
the only people in there. Did I mention we were there at
noon?

It was really kinda crazy. Sad, but crazy.

I walked in there one afternoon and who did I see? My
buddy's wife. Shit on a stick. Wow, did she rip me a new
asshole and, wow, did he throw me completely under the
bus. He said it was all my idea, I set up the girls, he wasn't
sure but he thought I worked there, he only went once,
blah, blah, blah. Later he told me that she saw a charge
on the credit card and he could think of no other way out
of it but to tell her that I had borrowed that money for
lap dances. He went so far with his lie that he made me
write him a check to pay him back. She basically told me
she was going to spread everything he told her around the
school and do everything in her power to make sure that I
wasn't back there the following year.

Her son was in my son's class so when I walked into
the principal's office for the meeting, I thought for sure the
principal was going to bring up my lunchtime escapades.
I sat down across from her and tried to throw a little humor in there to lighten up the mood. "Not sure what this is
about but I hope it doesn't have anything to do with all of
the drugs I'm selling at the school."

Wrong crowd.

She didn't even respond. In front of her, on her desk,

was my son Jacob's Scooby-Doo lunch box. She slowly pushed it across to me and said, "Would you open that, please?"

Wait a minute. Was I about to be critiqued on what I put in my son's lunch? Because that was not okay. I was particularly touchy about it because a lot of people who saw me with my kids just assumed that I didn't know what the fuck I was doing. When I was at the park, someone would inevitably tell me to "make sure your kids get plenty of fluids. It's really important." Really? Thank you so much, Captain Dumbass. Let me see if I can put this puzzle together all on my own. What you're saying is that kids are just like us and they need fluids so they won't dehydrate? I'm so glad you came along before my son dried up like a piece of beef jerky. It wasn't just in the park; it was everywhere. "You know, it's very important that you read to your children," someone told me at the library once. No shit? Good thing you told me because we were actually here because we're out of toilet paper at the house.

It was infuriating, so when the principal slid the lunch box over to me I was ready to go off. Jacob liked Yoo-Hoos so every now and then I'd pack him one. It's not the end of the world and I didn't need another person telling me about nutritional values and how kids are addicted to sugar and blah, blah, blah. They're kids. Let them eat a fucking Ding Dong. I pulled the lunch box closer to me and said, "I just want to let you know that I don't really appreciate your calling me in because you don't approve of what I give Jacob for lunch. He's a healthy kid. It's not like I load him up on caffeine and smokes."

The principal said nothing.

"Okay, I'm going to open this but I'm telling you right now, I'm not changing a thing. I know my son and I know what's best for him." Then I opened the lunch box and I saw...

...a full Budweiser.

Uh-oh.

"You were saying?" the principal quipped.

No, no, no, no, no. How did this happen? And then it all came back to me. Shit, shit, shit. When my brother and I were packing the lunches, I remember saying, "How funny would it be if he showed up to school with this in his lunch box?" And I put it in there. I guess I got so buzzed I forgot to take it out. Disaster. Absolute and utter disaster.

I looked at the principal and said, "I know how this looks."

"Do you?" she said.

"Maybe not," I answered. "Can I at least try to explain?"

"I think you should probably say something."

And I just told her the whole thing. I recently split with Jacob's mother and my brother and I had a few drinks after the kids went to sleep, and it was all just an innocent mistake. I really laid it on *thick*, knowing that the single-father thing worked on everyone. Except her apparently.

"Mr. Wolf, do you know how serious this is? You sent your four-year-old son to school with alcohol."

Well, put like that, it sounded pretty bad.

"Plus, it has come to my attention that you're working at a strip club near the school? Unless you can give me a good reason why I shouldn't, I'm afraid we're going to have to ask you to leave the preschool."

Holy shit balls. In my lifetime, I never thought that the people at the Jew School would have ever thought I was some guy who worked at a strip club near the school and who fed his four-year-old Bud in a can. Not gonna lie. I felt kinda badass for a second.

My buddy's angry wife must have told some grand story about how I lured helpless husbands to the local strip club and tricked them into getting boobs rubbed in their face because I was getting a piece of the action. Not true on all counts. Look, no straight man has to be talked into boobs. Boobs do all the talking they need to by themselves. Was I guilty of going to see noon titties?

Yes. Was I the first of the group to start going? Yes. But there was no way I could let Jacob get kicked out of the Jew School. Neither would I ever throw my buddy under the bus... but his wife?

Time to play the trump card.

Could she really have forgotten the day I saw her buying weed across the street from the school? She was sitting in her car and a guy pulled up next to her and made the transaction. I know, I know, it could have been anything—except it wasn't. How do I know? Because I bought weed from the same guy! And I know he sold her weed because I said to him, "Do you know you're on camera that close to the school?" and he said, "Fuck, really? I guess I won't be selling weed to that lady anymore." I think that was enough evidence. On top of that, after the transaction, she walked up to me and was extra nice. Too nice. She was asking why I didn't come over for dinner more, if she could set me up with some of her friends, and on and on. She never mentioned the weed—neither did I—and then things just slowly went back to normal, with her being a bitch.

I didn't want to get their son kicked out of school either so I said to the principal, "Can I make a quick phone call? I just want to get my brother on the phone so he can tell you the same story."

"That's not the biggest issue, Mr. Wolf."

One thing at a time. I stepped outside, called my brother, and then called my buddy's wife.

She was pretty holier than thou when she answered the phone and then I told her how it was going to be. I told her that if I was going down, she was going down with me. I would be okay. At least I could probably get some of the other guys to come to the principal's office and tell her I was no pimp. I could definitely get my brother down to the principal's office to tell her that I was going through a hard time, that we were just making a joke, and that it was an honest mistake. What could she do? Nothing. She could deny it all she wanted but it was on tape. She was fucked and she knew it.

I told her I was going back into the principal's office and if she didn't call within five minutes to say that my pimping was a lie, I was going to tell the principal that I saw her buying weed.

I waited thirty seconds and as I re-entered the office, the principal's phone rang. I was off the hook. I felt pretty damn good when I walked out of that school. I got in the car, cracked open that Budweiser, and drove straight to the strip club to celebrate.

P.S. To this day, boobs make me stop talking. I could be in the middle of a conversation with my wife and as soon as she takes her shirt off, it's like someone has pulled the plug on my brain. I have to fight myself from giggling and saying, "Boobies." They are so influential. It must be a great feeling to finally figure that out as a woman.

I remember the day I bought my daughter her first bra. I handed it to her and said, "You're like Spider-Man now. With great power comes great responsibility."

CHAPTER 9

Teenage Boys Are No Bueno

L et me start by saying that in no way am I interested in my daughter dating. Ever since my daughter was born, I've come to understand the whole arranged-marriage thing. You don't have to go through the dating and all that comes with it. Before you start sending me angry e-mails and burned bras, let me explain. It's not that I don't want my daughter to have a fun, healthy, regular life. I do. I just don't want it to involve penises. I know that dudes, especially teenage dudes, are lying scumbags and I say that with love and respect, having been one myself. It's not our fault. If women only knew how strong the testosterone pull is they wouldn't look at us like we're animals. It takes over sometimes and is truly uncontrollable. Have you ever seen someone get hypnotized at a show? Testosterone's just like that but worse. "Act like a chicken to get some pussy. Good. Now, go talk to that girl who's way out of your league so her and her friends can laugh at you while you walk away. Perfect!" It really is a burden.

I can hear women already. "We get just as horny as you. I don't know why men don't think we do." Uh, we think it because it's true. Much like we will never know what it's like to cramp, bloat, and be a hormonal mess once a month, you will never understand testosterone. I would say ninety percent of men in this country go through a fight/fuck stage. The fight/fuck stage is simple to explain. It's the attitude that "I'm either fucking tonight or fighting." And when you're young, there isn't really a huge difference between the two.

Let me give you an example.

When I was in high school, nothing assured me of vagina more than a two-liter bottle of Bartles and Jaymes wine coolers. Or better yet, Seagram's wine coolers. I can just hear Bruce Willis singing "Seagram's Golden Wine Coolers!" now. (Google it.) I was one of the guys who could access booze on a regular basis too. If my brother didn't buy it for me, I used one of his old IDs and either went to a little store in town or drove over the border to Vermont to load up. The place over the border was manned by the oldest person I have ever met in my entire life. This guy was old-old. Like three days older than baseball old. He wrote on parchment. His nuts were in a tomb. It took him ten minutes just to find the date of birth on the ID. And he always said the same thing. "Who am I kidding? You could be eight years old and I would never know. I can't even see my willy when I take a leak. Gotta do it by feel, ya know?" That's nice. Can you just sell me my panty-dropping juice? I have to drive home and coax someone into have sex with me.

One night my buddy and I were in the woods with these two girls. That was our "date." Nobody's parents were out of town so there were no house parties. Neither my buddy nor I could get a car for the night, and the girls weren't old enough to drive so we were stuck walking. And in high school, for those of us who lived near them, the woods were always the backup plan.

So into the woods we went with two blankets, two two-liter bottles of wine coolers, a bottle of Jack Daniels, and the knowledge that there was a good chance that one of us might see some Vinny J. We would have walked into woods full of wasps that stung people in the eyeballs with acid if there was a chance that one of us might see some Vanana. High school is the "smell my finger" time of your life, so if you don't get any and your friend does, it's almost just as good. (Women don't have anything like that. Women never touch a dude's balls and go, "Get a whiff of this guy!")

Anyway, we were in the woods and things were going

according to plan. My buddy had taken his girl, one of the blankets, and one of the wine coolers to his own little spot and I had all the ingredients for my witches brew with me. My girl, who couldn't pronounce her Rs and whose name was Beth, was a girl I had tried to hook up with before.

I say tried because I actually had her at my house one night when my parents weren't home and could have sealed the deal for sure but her breath was so bad I couldn't make it happen. I know that sounds crazy but it's true. I didn't want to get near her face, but she wouldn't have sex with me unless I kissed her. Not totally unreasonable, I guess, but there was *no way* I could do it. And I tried everything that night. I even took her into the kitchen and tried to get her to eat a spoonful of peanut butter. I figured if peanut butter couldn't kill that dragon breath, nothing could. Problem was, she was a drunk, horny teenager who didn't want to eat peanut butter. The only thing she wanted to eat were Doritos. Yeah, those will make the breath better for sure. Yuck.

For weeks after that fiasco, Beth felt rejected because I wouldn't kiss her. She wouldn't go out with me because she thought that since I turned my head every time she came toward me, I must have been disgusted by her. Not true. I loved her boobies. I was disgusted by the nine-year-old piece of cheese she must have been hiding under her tongue. The situation wasn't helped by that fact that my friends and I started calling her "Bweth."

Talking her into the woods required some planning and a promise that we would kiss and, after all the lying and reassuring, there we were on the blanket. She was guzzling wine coolers and I was drinking Jack Daniels and shoveling gum into my mouth and getting ready for the holy unknown. I knew she was talking because her mouth was moving and sounds were coming out of it but what she was saying wasn't registering at all. All I could think about was how to close the deal.

When I could tell she was drunk enough to forget she was in the woods and I was drunk enough not to notice the smell of rancid ass coming out of her mouth, I made my move. I figured if I went in fast for the kiss, I might be able to catch her before she exhaled. Unfortunately, I wasn't that lucky. When I was about three inches from her face she burped and out of her mouth came the smell of warm death. It coated my face like a mask and stunned me like I had just been head-butted.

I think if I had been older than twenty-one, I would have packed up my shit and left. There would have been no way I could have continued to take that kind of punishment. But my hormones propped me back up and took over. They said, "You are going to grab a boob tonight and at the very least do some serious dry humping. Now, pull your shit together and get back in there!" And I did. As soon as I saw her inhale I attacked her face again. I never gave her an opportunity to breathe out, and with the twenty-seven pieces of gum I was chewing on, I officially cancelled out the hot death that was pouring out of her grill.

I thought I was in for sure. We were lying on the blanket, I had already grabbed a boob (after a twelve-minute struggle with her bra. Man, they should go over that in sex ed), and there was smoke coming from the intense dry-humping friction our jeans were generating. It was awesome. And right when I thought about trying to maneuver a little below-the-belt action I felt a huge pain in my right calf. I tried to push through it but it started spreading up my leg and pretty soon I just couldn't take it anymore.

It takes *a lot* for a sixteen-year-old guy to stop rolling around with a girl. *A lot.* I turned over on my shoulder and it looked like the blanket was alive. I looked closer and I could see them...ants. And they were crawling all over me. I turned to tell Bweth what was happening and when I did...*Bam!* She threw up in my face. Shit.

Apparently, when I looked over my shoulder at the ants, I dropped my body weight on Bweth's stomach. A stomach that was filled with wine coolers. Drenched in a Berry-Berry nightmare, I jumped up and started slapping at the back of my leg. It must have taken a good five minutes to get all the ants off me and longer to remove Bartles and Jaymes from the inside of my nose. I took my sweatshirt off, shook out the blanket, and, wouldn't you know it, I was still horny.

Getting bit by ants and thrown up on wasn't enough torment for my little general to stand down. I think that's when I truly knew who was running the show. Testosterone kicked back in and convinced me that, what the hell, her breath couldn't be any worse, right?

Much to my disappointment, vomiting was not on Bweth's list of foreplay activities so the night ended there. Did I mention that I don't want my daughter around teenage boys?

That being said, I don't want to stop my daughter from dating during high school because we've all seen what happens to girls who don't date when they finally leave the house. Wow. And let me just say to the parents of those girls, on behalf of all freshmen boys at colleges all around the country: *Thank you!* Nothing is off limits with those chicks. Who knew that anal while eating pizza and wearing a caveman costume was even an option?

Is it wrong that I don't want my daughter to date but I want my son to have sex with as many girls as he can? As a father, I get a crazy sense of pride knowing that my oldest son is taking care of business. Not in a dirty-old-man kinda way but in a that's-my-boy kinda way. Honestly, it's just another thing that grown men can compete about.

And let me tell you, if your son is the kid who's getting the most ass—winner!

Better yet is if your son is the kid who gets "busted" for sleeping with the teacher. Holy shit! You might get a trophy for that one. That tops valedictorian, captain of the football team, full ride to Harvard, and whatever else is out there. Bangin' the teacher is *way* better. I'll also tell you this: I think they should be a little more lenient on the female teachers who get arrested for having sex with male students. They paint them out to be these crazy predators who ruin kids' lives when nothing could be further from the truth. Are you kidding me?

First of all, that kid is now a hero among his friends. He instantly turns into the coolest kid in the school. Second, and more important, girls who never paid attention to him before are gonna wanna have sex with him because they will instantly assume that he knows what he's doing. It's a win-win.

He won't know what he's doing, by the way. No amount of teaching can show a teenage boy what to do in bed. He's way too excited just to be there to try to follow any kind of rules or regulations.

Lastly, the idea of this woman being a predator is crazy.

He's already had sex with her fifty-eight times in his head...along with every other girl who's walking those hallways. *He's* the predator. At that age, *he's* the animal.

That leads me right back to why I don't want teenage boys around my daughter.

And the one big thing I hadn't taken into account: the Internet. It wasn't something my parents had to deal with; in fact, we are the first generation of parents who have had to figure out how to manage Twitter, Facebook, and every other social networking/pedophile outlet on the web. The craziest thing about these sites to me is that my daughter had met some of her "best friends" on there. Uh, attention, clueless generation, if you're meeting your best friends online then you've never actually met your best friends! They could be some dude I went to college with.

"No, they're not, Dad. See the picture?"

Uh, attention, clueless generation, that might not be their picture.

It really was a tough situation. One thing I decided early on was that my kids were not going to grow up the way I did. I was not going to be just like my dad, who couldn't figure out why we needed a remote control for the TV. "You can just get up and turn it." Or you could get a remote control and stay on the couch.

Of course, I wanted my kids to do what the other kids

their age were doing. I wanted them to be part of their freaky, no-human-contact generation where kids no longer make eye contact or actually speak words to each other. It's their rite of passage.

At the same time, with my daughter getting interested in boys, I had to figure out a way to monitor what she did online without being intrusive. So I did what every other mature adult would do. I hacked her passwords. Don't judge me. I figured it was the best way to get what I wanted while still giving her "freedom." She and I sat down, talked about what I wanted the rules to be (no giving out a phone number, location, or real name, and no talk that would make me throw up in my mouth were the main ones), and off she went.

About a month into the experiment, my daughter was officially obsessed and she had found her "soul mate."

"Oh, my God, Daddy. I love him so much."

I knew for sure it wasn't her soul mate but I try to have my kids learn things themselves rather than tell them what I know to be true. After all, no matter how many times someone tells a child that something's hot, they don't really figure it out until they touch it. Let them experience it before telling them they shouldn't do it. It's a huge part of my parenting philosophy.

After a few months of "talking" online, she finally asked

me if they could talk on the phone. Actual almost human contact. A big step for this generation. I told her to give me the phone number and I would call so I could talk to the kid and his parents.

"Oh, my god, Daddy. Thank you sooooooo much! I love him!"

Whatever.

When I called, she was sitting next to me, a bundle of teenage energy, squeezing one of her stuffed animals. "Don't embarrass me, Daddy. Just make sure he is who he says he is, talk to his mom, and get off the phone."

It never fails. No matter how cool you think you are, you are always an embarrassment to your kids. I look around at some of the other fathers and think, "My kids have to think I'm cooler than that dude." Nope. They think I am the biggest dork to ever walk the earth. And because of that, to torture them, every now and then I act really stupid in public. I'm not saying I act silly. I literally pretend to be the stupidest person on the face of the planet. Funny for me, not so much for them.

So I called the number and this was what I got:

"Hello?" Imagine a typical teenage boy's voice. You know how they all sound. Like Edward Furlong from *Terminator 2.*

"Hey, this is Josh, Kaitlynn's father. Is Garrett there?"

"Yeah."

Uncomfortable three beats of silence.

"Is this Garrett?"

"Yeah."

"Hey, I know Kaitlynn wanted to talk to you on the phone and I just wanted to make sure you were who you said you were, ya know?"

"Yeah."

Uncomfortable three beats of silence.

"Okay. Is your mom or dad there? I want to make sure it's okay with them, too."

And here was where the real funny started.

"Yeah, hold on. Mom! (Beat) Mom! (Beat) Hold on, she's on the other side of the trailer."

What? I'm sorry, what? First of all, how big was that fucking trailer? *Other side of the trailer?* Did that mean he couldn't just nudge her with his foot? And before I could say anything, I got this beauty.

"Mom! Would you put down the Taco Bell for once? Kaitlynn's dad wants to talk to you!"

Put down the Taco Bell *for once*? That meant this kid had been snubbed by Taco Bell more than once in his life? And before I could mentally digest that...

"Oh, for God's sake, Mom, you have hot sauce all over your shirt."

And it was at that very moment that one of my daily inner battles reared its ugly head. This was clearly not the home situation that I envisioned my daughter walking into. An extra-large trailer where the mom placed grilled stuffed burritos ahead of her children wasn't exactly on my wish list. On the other hand, as a comedian, I kinda wanted to play this out.

It happens in my life all of the time. I end up in situations that are bad for me because I just can't walk away from the crazy. It's how I got my one and only stalker. I was at the dog park in Los Angeles and this woman started talking to me about how September 11th happened because of a video the government took of her masturbating in front of her TV. She had me at hello. I couldn't turn away from that shit. Little did I know that just by talking to her she would decide that I was just like Sandra Oh and Tom Cruise, who apparently had been trying to steal her identity and her artwork since the mid-nineties.

Back to the phone call...The next thing I heard was chewing and breathing and chewing and breathing.

"Hello?"

"Hi, I'm Josh, Kaitlynn's father."

Heavy breathing. "Yeah?"

"Uh, I was just checking to see if it was okay with you if the kids talked on the phone?"

"Uh-huh, why wouldn't it be?"

"Well, uh, I just wanted you to know that your son is

actually talking to a teenage girl and not some forty-eight-year-old man."

"Forty-eight-year-old man? Why would he be doing that? What are you, some kind of pervert?"

"Me? No! I'm saying my daughter isn't a pervert."

"Daddy!"

"Sorry, princess." Back into the phone: "So, you're okay with it?"

"Yup."

And that was it. The next few weeks were my own private hell. My daughter walked around the house and all she could talk about was "Garrett, Garrett, Garrett. I am so in love with Garrett, Daddy. He is so amazing!"

You... have... never... met him!

I thought I had made the biggest mistake in the world. I mean, how could I ever prove to her that she was wrong and that the world she had created in her head was one giant lie? And then it happened. Some may call it divine intervention but I just called it dumb luck. I booked a gig in Bumfuck, which coincidentally was not too far from where Garrett lived.

I told my wife that I was going to take Kaitlynn with me to meet Garrett. That way she could see for herself that she was living in a dream world and she would understand that relationships you make that are purely online can't be trusted. We would come home and she would throw away her computer, swear off boys, and remain a virgin until the day I died. I thought it was a pretty solid plan.

My wife asked, "Are you stupid?"

Not the response I was looking for.

"Do you know nothing about teenage girls? You are bringing her out there and she is going to fall *more* in love. It's her first love."

And then she said something that scared the shit out of me. She said, "If she goes and this guy turns out to be the love of her life, your credibility is shot. From this day forward, anytime you say, 'Trust me. I know what I'm talking about,' she will laugh in your face. Are you willing to risk that?"

It was a great question, and a huge risk, but what I kept going back to was the picture Garrett had sent of "himself." As a guy, I gave him credit because he probably figured that the only person who would see that picture was Kaitlynn and maybe some of her friends. There was no way he could think that she would show her father, who would recognize a Photoshopped picture of Johnny Depp from *21 Jump Street*. Can you believe that shit? The kid had the balls to Photoshop a picture of Johnny fucking Depp! I was starting to like him more and more. I also had some experience with the Net and knew from what I saw with Twitter and Facebook, the people I "talked" to online and the ones who showed up at my shows looked like two entirely different people. I was willing to take the risk.

I walked into my daughter's room and said, "How would you like to meet Garrett?"

She said, "I've already met him. What are you talking about?"

Ugh. "What I meant was, how would you like to meet him in person?"

And that was when the freak-out started. Maybe the biggest teenage freak ever. "Oh. My. God. Are you serious? Please tell me you're serious. This is the best day ever and you are the best dad in the entire world!" I think that was followed by about eighty-seven "Oh, my Gods" and seven or eight dolphin noises.

As I was planning the trip, a little nugget of information came out that threw me for a bit of a loop. Kaitlynn confided in me (and now I'm telling it to the whole world) that she had never kissed anyone before and wanted Garrett to be her first. Wow. I wasn't sure exactly where to put that one. Part of me thought it was awesome that she felt comfortable telling me and how cool it would be that we could share that momentous occasion. And the other part of me started to think that it was a little weird that I was flying my daughter halfway across the country to make out with some stranger. Just typing that makes me feel like Child

Protective Services might knock on my door at any second. I finally decided that, even though the thought of my daughter locking lips with some dude made me want to vomit, this was about as safe and controlled an environment as I could hope for. We moved forward.

When the day came she was a complete spaz. Carrying her stuffed animal, Mudpie, muttering about eight thousand OMGs, and telling everyone (and I mean *everyone*) who came within two feet of us, "I'm going to see my boyfriend Garrett. I'm going to marry him." It was like Tourette's on crack.

The plane ride was equally painful and, even though I put my headphones on and closed my eyes, she continued talking. At one point, she got up to go to the bathroom and the guy in the aisle seat looked at me and said, "Is she too young for Xanax?"

When we landed, we went straight to the rental car place. The guy behind the counter was way too happy to see us. I gave him my last name and he said, "Mr. Wolf, it says here that you've reserved a Taurus. Are you sure you don't want to get a convertible for you and your lady friend?"

Lady friend? Both Kaitlynn and I were stunned for a second, and then she said, "Ugh! That's my dad!"

We got the car for free.

When we got to our hotel room, we looked out the window and saw that the local high school was having its prom in the back parking lot. You read that right. In the parking lot. I could tell right away that it was going to be a special night. We got ourselves ready for the show and drove over to the venue.

Kaitlynn and I waited out front for Garrett and his father. Kaitlynn had the *21 Jump Street* picture out and was looking for Johnny Depp. I was not. She kept glancing down at the picture and back up saying, "No. That's not him. That's not him either. I don't see him anywhere, Daddy." And I was thinking, "That's true because you're not gonna see the guy in that picture anywhere near here tonight."

As the arena started to fill up, I could see Kaitlynn was getting a little worried and that's when I saw them. I didn't know for sure it was them but something inside me said it was. Like in a movie when the crowd splits and the stars of the film show up and walk toward the camera in slow motion? Well, it was nothing like that. What I saw coming toward me was better and worse than I could have possibly imagined. Worse because it was my baby girl and I didn't want her to be disappointed but better because I love being right. And I was.

First of all, Garrett looked nothing like Johnny Depp. He looked more like Johnny Don't. He was pale, pale, pale. I mean pale. He made Nicole Kidman look like Flava

Flav. He was pale. He looked like he stepped in a pail of pale he was so pale. I could see his brain. That's how pale he was. He had the typical greasy long, teenager hair that fell into his eyes. Not sure how to describe his clothes but they were a crazy blend of Marilyn Manson and Toby Keith. And he had *the biggest* zit I have ever seen. It almost looked like he had a tit on his chin.

He walked right up to my daughter and said, "Kaitlynn?" Kaitlynn looked at him, looked down at his picture, looked back up at him, and said in disbelief, "Garrett?" They stared awkwardly at each other for a second and then hugged even more awkwardly. Man, being a teenager blows. As they hugged, Garrett's father stuck his hand out and said, "Name's Steve. Pleased to meet you."

Now, when I refer to teeth and what I like to call "the front eight," most of you don't really know what I'm talking about because you have all of them. Steve did not. Steve had one. A tooth. And it wasn't just one tooth; it was the single longest tooth in the history of the world. No wonder he didn't have the other ones, all the calcium in his body had gone to that one slot. I bet the tooth fairy sat outside of his window every night just looking at it and thinking, "Damn! There's no way I'll have enough money for that thing!" When Steve dies, they will be able to grab his feet and use him as a garden hoe is all I'm saying.

Steve and I stepped back for a second to let the kids talk and he said, "Garrett's never had a girlfriend before." No shit? It looks like Garrett's never been outside before. But I bet his cleric is level forty-five, isn't it? Steve and I talked a little more and he was a super nice guy but it was real clear, real fast, that we didn't share a whole lot of common interests, like toothpaste and vitamins.

By this point the show was about to start, so I suggested that they go to their seats and we would meet up afterward.

I pulled Kaitlynn aside just to make sure she was still into it and she said, "He doesn't look exactly the same but he's my soul mate, Daddy. I know he is."

I said, "So, you guys are having some good conversation?"

"Not really. But I think that's just because we're both nervous."

And because he'd never talked to an actual live girl before.

She assured me that she was going to be fine and went to sit down with Steve and Garrett. I could see them from the stage and it was kinda cool watching my daughter in the audience. Not only was I actually making her laugh but it was the first time I caught a glimpse of her as an adult. It was a moment in my life I will never forget.

After the show, we got to the front of the arena and I pulled Kaitlynn aside to ask her how things were going.

"He's not exactly the same as I thought he was," she said.

"So should we call it a night?" I asked.

"Not yet."

"Are you still looking for that first kiss?"

She nodded.

"Okay, well then let's have some dinner," I suggested.

We walked over to Steve and Garrett and I told them to pick any type of food they wanted for dinner, my treat. That's when I heard one of the greatest words I had ever heard in my life. I'd heard the word before but it had never made me quite as happy as it did that night.

Steak. Steve wanted to eat steak. Let me rephrase that. One-Tooth Steve wanted to eat steak. As a person who will go to the ends of the earth to see things he's never seen before, this was a dream come true. How the fuck was he going to eat steak?

When Kaitlynn and I got in the car that was all I could talk about. I was trying to figure out Steve's steak-eating method. "Do you think he'll cut it into tiny little pieces and swallow them whole? Wait, maybe he puts the pieces in his mouth and stores them like a squirrel stores a nut. Oh, I know! He gets Garrett to chew it for him and he just swallows it!" I was obsessed.

229

We sat down at dinner and, boy, I couldn't order those steaks fast enough. Bring the appetizers and the entrees together! Let's get this show started! As we waited for the food to come and Kaitlynn and Garrett had less and less to say to each other, it was up to me and Steve to carry the conversation. Steve really loved his kids and it was clear that the road trip to see Kaitlynn was an extravagance, but he was willing to do it for his kid. I respected that. Really did. And I wish I could have told him that but all I heard when he was talking was, "Blah, blah, blah" because I could not fucking wait for that steak to come out! Right when I thought I was going to explode, our waiter sidled up next to the table and started handing out the food.

The anticipation was killing me and I'll be damned if Steve didn't start on his mashed potatoes first. It was torture. I tried to listen in on the conversation between Kaitlynn and Garrett but I couldn't do that either because they were done talking. Kaitlynn had even stopped trying. She wasn't being rude, but instead of trying to manufacture conversation like she had all night, she just sat there silently, smiling politely.

Right before I stood on my chair and screamed, "For the love of all that's holy, eat the fucking steak already!" it happened. Steve was right in the middle of telling me about how he had met his wife when the fork and knife first touched the meat. It was like time stopped around me and all I could see was Steve and his meat. I was mesmerized.

As the first bite went up to his mouth, I thought, "There goes my theory about Garrett chewing it for him." As the fork entered his mouth, I couldn't wait to see what was going to happen next. It wasn't an unusually small piece of meat on the fork and he hadn't done anything special to it beforehand so, for the life of me, I couldn't figure out how he was going to eat that thing. And then... it happened.

I'd heard about a million times in my life that the tongue, pound for pound, is the strongest muscle in your body. I guess if you have no teeth, your tongue would have to be even stronger. When Steve put the piece of steak in, he *mashed* it against the roof of his mouth with his tongue and then swallowed it, all in one motion. It was amazing.

For me, the trip was already a total and complete success.

By the end of dinner, I wasn't sure if Kaitlynn wanted this charade to go on any longer. She didn't dislike Garrett, but through no fault of his own, he wasn't who she thought he'd be. I paid for the meal (which was worth every single last penny) and Kaitlynn and I told the two of them that we would meet them in the parking lot.

When I asked her if she wanted to end the night there or still try to get that first kiss, you could see the anguish on her face. She didn't see herself and Garrett as soul mates anymore, but she had come all this way to get her first kiss. I reminded her that you only get one first kiss, so she should make sure this was how she wanted to remember it. She had a completely different outlook on it. Almost a "What happens in Vegas stays in Vegas" point of view.

She figured that she might as well get a little of the nerves and awkwardness out of the way so that when she kissed someone for real, she'd be a little better at it. Plus, since none of her friends were there they would never have to know what happened. And if she did tell them, she could make Garrett be whoever she wanted him to be. She still wanted the kiss and, for the record, I totally respected that decision.

When Steve and Garrett met us in the parking lot, I suggested that we all go back to our hotel to talk some more. They both liked the idea and, before they could walk to the car, I pulled Steve aside to tell him what the deal was.

"Listen," I said. "Kaitlynn and Garrett want a little time alone if that's okay with you."

"That's fine with me," Steve said a little too enthusiastically. "Is it okay with you?"

"It's fine. It's not like we're sending them up to my hotel room. There are a couple of chairs next to the elevators where they can hang while you and I sit in the lobby."

The drive back was interesting for me and Kaitlynn, to say the least. I was assuming it wasn't too often that a father flew his daughter halfway around the country to get her first kiss. I was also assuming it wasn't too often that the father was stuck in an awkward situation where he felt he had to say something about it. I mean, it wasn't that I felt I had to tell her how to kiss or give her instructions. That would have made me drive my car off a cliff.

I just felt something had to be said to acknowledge the occasion. Something meaningful but that didn't put a lot of pressure on either of us. And how I wish I had come up with something fitting. Instead I came up with this beauty: "Good thing he's got more teeth than his dad or you wouldn't be kissing, you'd be gumming."

Not a winner.

After sufficiently blowing my chance for a nice father-daughter moment, we pulled into the hotel and met Garrett and Steve in the lobby. I told the kids that we would be sitting in the lobby and that they were to go to the chairs by the elevators. They had fifteen minutes and the clock started...now.

The two of them ran out of the lobby, leaving me and Steve sitting on two chairs that faced each other. Before I could say a word, he started the conversation with this: "I was in a coma for six months."

I wish I was in a fucking coma right now. "Really? What happened?"

"Daddy ran over me with a tractor."

Now I'm interested. "No shit?"

"Yeah. When I woke up he said he was real, real sorry."

In about two seconds I had gone from wanting to figure out how to fake a heart attack in order to get out of there to never wanting to leave. I *love* stories like that. Right when it was starting to get interesting, Kaitlynn and Garrett were back. I looked at my watch—only ten minutes had gone by.

"You've got another five minutes, Princess," I told her.

"I know," she said. "I'm ready to go upstairs now."

"You don't want your five minutes?" I asked.

"No, thank you."

Something was up because she really wanted to go. Before I had even stood up, she had said good-bye to Steve and Garrett and walked out of the lobby. I shook both of their hands, told them it was great meeting them, and hoped they had a safe trip home.

Steve pulled me to the side and said, "I want you to know we had a great time and can't wait to come see you guys in California." Uh...never gonna happen. Super nice guy. Never, ever gonna happen.

When I got to the elevators, Kaitlynn was waiting for me, silent. She didn't say a word on the way up to the room, didn't say a word as she was getting ready for bed, and just stared at the TV from her bed as I pretended not to notice that she wasn't talking.

When I couldn't take it anymore, I said, "Nothing? We flew all this way, planned out this whole night, and you're giving me nothing?"

Kaitlynn slowly turned to me, propped herself up on her elbows, and said, "What do you want to know?"

"Uh...let's start with everything! Are you kidding me right now? You were gone for only ten minutes so it can't be too much to tell, right?"

She sat up, brushed some imaginary crumbs from her bed, and said, "Okay, well, we sat down on the chairs next to the elevator and started talking about how neither one of us had ever kissed someone before."

Not a huge shock.

"So we thought it would be cool if we were each other's firsts. Uh, so...like, we leaned in, but we leaned in too fast? Ya know? And my chin popped his zit."

Excuse me? Did she just say that her chin popped his zit? I didn't know whether to laugh, cry, throw up in my bed, or hose her down. Popped his zit with her chin? I've farted during sex, I've pooped my pants on a first date, I've even asked a girl if she minded if I turned on a Red Sox game while she was blowing me because it was the playoffs. But there is no coming back from your zit popping on someone else's face. That is the deal breaker of all deal breakers. I almost felt bad for the kid.

Almost.

Because what raced past the feeling of sympathy was the sweet taste of victory. This trip had turned out to be a complete and unabashed success. I got to pretend to be the cool dad by bringing Kaitlynn to get her first kiss, and she saw me perform and for a second almost looked like she was a little proud of me. And I saw a man with one tooth eat steak, and Kaitlynn learned firsthand that the Internet does not always spout the truth.

The best thing about the trip actually turned out to be the bond that Kaitlynn and I developed over the weekend. We'd always been close, but sharing that experience and having her talk to me about her feelings was something I never thought I would have with her. I was actually her sounding board. Crazy.

After she told me about the zit, there was a very silent moment. Probably where the "Oh, my God! That is the grossest fucking thing I have ever heard!" should have gone.

"I'm really sorry," I said (a lie).

"Thanks, Daddy." (Beat) "Do you know what the weirdest thing is?"

"What's that, Princess?"

"After he cleaned off his chin, he tried to kiss me again!
Can you believe that?"

Yes, I can. Boys are disgusting.

CHAPTER 10

Wrestling with the Future

There's a point in every boy's life when he looks at his father and says to himself, "I think I can fuckin' take that guy." It usually happens right around the time the kid has so many hormones coursing through him that zits actually form while he's washing his face. It doesn't take much to trigger it either because a teenage boy has a worse temper than that awful tub of a woman who teaches little girls to dance on TLC. The trigger is usually something innocuous like being asked to take out the trash. The kid walks away mumbling, "If that old motherfucker asks me to take out the trash one more time I seriously might beat his ass." The alpha male always gets challenged. For me and my son, it was no different.

In the back of my mind I was waiting for the day. I could see it coming slowly but surely. Every day he got a little mouthier, a little braver, and he started walking around the house with his shirt off. When a guy walks around with his shirt off all of the time, it's for one of two reasons: he's either really happy with the way his body looks or he's drunk and about to be on an episode of *Cops*. Not sure why, but when guys get drunk, shirts come off. In college, it wasn't just shirts either. A few of us always ended up naked and standing around the keg with straw hats on and extra large cups in our hands.

Though I was pretty sure my son wasn't at the absolute tipping point yet, the push-ups he'd been doing at night had started to fill him up with a little extra courage.

And then it happened.

I was walking through the kitchen one morning and he just…leaned his shoulder into me. Nothing big enough to knock me over but just enough to push me off course a little bit. I turned to him and said, "Did you just lean your shoulder into me?"

"If I leaned my shoulder into you, you'd know it," he said. "Maybe you should just watch where you're going."

Uh-oh. "Are you…picking a fight with me?"

"No."

"I hope not," I said.

"Why? Because you know I'd win?"

"You think you'd win?" I asked.

"I know I'd win," he said. "You don't want any of this, old timer."

Old timer? Well I had to fight him now. "Let's go," I said as I tightened up my shoelaces and headed for the front door.

"Now?"

"Yeah, now."

"I'm not ready right now and we're not fighting, we're wrestling. Two weeks. Give me two weeks and you are going down!"

"You're going to train? Who are you? Rocky?" I asked.

"Who's Rocky?"

Did he say "Who's Rocky?" Well, now I had to kick his ass for real. I told him two weeks was fine by me and he stormed out of the room.

But as much as I made fun of him for suggesting two weeks, I was thinking "Phew." I don't know about anyone else but I'm at that age where I pull muscles. I needed two weeks to make sure I wouldn't pull a hammy in the first thirty seconds of the match. About a week earlier I had pulled a muscle in my shoulder while—are you ready for this?—wiping my ass. I guess I reached back a little too quickly or maybe I didn't rotate my torso enough, but I fucked myself up for weeks just trying to clean the pooper.

You know you're getting old when you have to stretch out before you take a dump.

I had to strategize a little bit. I remember wrestling my

father when I was a kid so I thought I'd start with a phone call to him to pick his brain about the situation. My father had lived through three boys before me so surely I wasn't the only one who had flexed his nuts and tried to wrestle him down. He had to be a wealth of information.

"Oh, I remember that," he said. "All of you tried to fight me."

And?

"And all of you lost."

"I remember it ended kinda quickly," I said. "You weren't messing around at all."

"Oh, yeah. I don't know what kind of shape you think you're in, but wrestling is really hard. I knew that I had a minute at the most before I would have been winded."

He was right. I work out but not like I used to. A minute of wrestling would tire me out for sure. Shit, when I have sex with my wife, I always tell her, "I want you to get on top. You look so beautiful up there." I really should just be saying, "Can't you see me sweating on top of you? Do some work! I'm fucking winded here."

He went on to give me a couple of moves that worked on all of us and reminded me that teenagers wrestle like a jack in the box. They come out of the gate fast and strong but they have no plan or direction. Then my father said something that really hit home. He said, "The biggest thing to remember is that he wants to win, right?"

"Right."

"But you . . . you *have* to win."

He was right. Can you imagine what would happen if he won? The next time I told him to do anything, he would just tell me to go fuck myself or he'd beat my ass again and then I'd have to shoot him and bury him in the backyard. I couldn't let that happen so I started to plan.

What did I have over him? Physically he may not have been stronger but for sure he could last more than a minute. I really thought that if it came down to just physical stuff, I was going to be in a lot of trouble. I had to rely on the mental. You know why? Because teenagers are stupid. Especially teenage boys.

What other group of people think it's funny to light their taints on fire and put it on YouTube? Is there another crowd that punches each other in the nuts and laughs? How can you not think that people who watch their friends take catastrophic spills on their skateboards and stand around and laugh instead of helping aren't a tiny bit retarded? For the record, I think all three of those things are really funny. Not sure what that says about me exactly.

I knew that in order for me to guarantee victory, I had to start mental warfare immediately and I couldn't let up until he snapped. I refused to lose.

As I planned and plotted, Beth sat down next to me and said, "What are you doing?"

"Planning victory."

"Okay. You know you're ridiculous, right?"

I wasn't expecting that at all. Was she on his side? What about through thick and thin, for better or worse, and all that other shit?

"Just tell him that you're the adult, this is your house, and you're not fighting. I can't believe you're actually planning on going through with this. You're the grown-up. Act like one."

Nuh-uh.

Clearly Beth, who hadn't grown up around boys, didn't understand how things worked. My son basically took his nuts out in the kitchen that day, and I had to do the same thing. I don't think women understand that shit because they're more evolved than we are. When I'm driving on the freeway and someone cuts me off, I *have* to pull in front of them and cut them off in return. Have to. I race people on the freeway all of the time, and they have no idea they're even part of the race but at some point they passed me so in my mind it's on!

My son had challenged me. I couldn't back down from a challenge, no matter how ridiculous and petty it was. And the thought that Beth expected me to was equally ridiculous. You know who does that? Uh...grown-ups! I never

243

act like a grown-up and I'm not sure I ever will. Hell, my father is almost seventy-five years old and he still thinks fart jokes are funny.

My son and I were going to wrestle.

And I was going to kick his ass. Not hurt him. That was never the plan. The plan was to let him know who the alpha dog of this pack still was.

"Fine," Beth said. "But this is not going to end well."

Yeah, I know. For him.

As he prepared physically for the match, I started the mental warfare. I began by taking all of his underwear out of his drawer and replacing them with panties. Not just any panties, but the panties that had the days of the week on them. The first day he woke up and found them, he went nuts!

"Hey!" I heard him scream from his room. "What the...? Who took my underwear?"

"What's wrong, buddy?"

"You know what's wrong! You took my underwear!"

"I have no idea what you're talking about. Come on out here and show me."

"I'm not showing you because *you know* what I'm talking about!"

"Do I?" I asked.

"You think this bothers me? This doesn't bother me. You can't bother me!"

Okay. Whatever you say. "Just put your Mondays on, sunshine, and come on out and grab some breakfast."

"I'm not wearing panties!!! This doesn't bother me!!! You can't bother me!!!"

This was gonna be too easy.

The next thing I did to drive him a little crazy was put the theme song to *Rocky* on every iPod, iPhone, and iPad in the house. When he was in his room doing push-ups, I would put an iPod against the door and play that song. He would open up his door and scream, "That doesn't bother me! You still can't bother me!"

Ah, music to my ears.

I know I shouldn't have been getting so much joy from fucking with him, but it truly was awesome. I did stupid things like short-sheet his bed and put Tabasco sauce on the inside rim of his hats, and they brought me more joy than I care to admit. All along, Beth would just look at me and shake her head. "This isn't going to end well," she repeated.

Uh...wasn't she watching? It seemed to be going pretty fucking well so far.

The best thing I did, the absolute masterpiece, was when I put online a video of him from when he was about five years old. In the video, he was wearing a black top hat...and that was it. He was pretending to be a magician, and his magic trick was tucking his little ding-dong between his legs and making it disappear. Incredibly cute when you're five. Death when you're a teenager and all of your friends have the Internet in the palm of their hands.

The video didn't actually get that many hits. But it got all of the right ones. How did I know that? Because he came home one day screaming, "Very funny, old man! Very funny! I could put up with the panties and the stupid *Rocky* music. I could even put up with the Tabasco. I thought that was pretty funny. But putting that video online is the end! Do you hear me? The end! Me and you are going outside on the lawn...NOW!" He walked into his room and slammed the door.

I think I got to him.

Beth walked in and said, "What the hell was all that?"

"He heard about the video."

"You are a child," she said. "Whatever happens after this, do not ask me for help. Do you hear me? I'm not helping you." And she walked out.

Girls. What do they know about stupid immature stuff? Nothin'. That's what.

The way I had planned out this scene in my head, he would get mad and I would have until the next day to stretch. But the way he stormed into his room, I had fifteen minutes at best. I immediately started stretching my hamstrings. They were the key. If my hamstrings were loose, it always seemed like my whole body was loose.

I hadn't done two stretches before my son came out of his room. He was wearing shorts, a bandana, and...no shirt.

You heard me.

"Are we going to wrestle or Abercrombie and Fitch?" I said.

"Let's do this!" my son said as he walked past me to the front yard.

I followed and saw him on the lawn doing these... running dance stretch poses, I guess is what I'd call them. He looked ridiculous.

"Are you ready?" he said.

"For what?" I answered honestly. I mean, I honestly had no idea what he was planning to do. Those stretch moves weren't athletic in any sense of the word.

"To wrestle."

At that point in my life, this was by far the most white trash thing I had ever thought to do: wrestling my shirtless son on the front lawn of my house with my other two kids watching. The only pieces missing to complete this dysfunctional puzzle were a family member on meth and a big tub of Mac-n-Cheese. My neighbor actually poked his head out of his door and said, "Everything okay, Josh?"

"Go back in your house, Alan," I said, waving to him.

As Alan went back inside, I nodded my head to my son, basically saying, "Bring it, bitch." And he did. A couple of things became painfully clear when he charged me. One, he obviously had never been in a fight before because he ran at me like a one-armed, two-fingered, brain-damaged monkey. The other thing was that he was fucking serious. He had this look in his eye like he was about to pay me back for every dish I had made him wash, every trash bag I had made him take out, and every piece of laundry I had made him wash. EV-ER-Y-THING. Everything he had ever wanted to say to me was balled up in this one moment...and I was about to squash it.

He was coming fast but was completely out of control so I grabbed his arm and flipped him over my back. *Whoomp.* He fell square on his back. You ever land flat on your back and hear that *puuuuuuhhhhhh-puuuuuhhhhh* noise come out of you? All of the air just shoots out of your mouth and you get the wind knocked out of you.

One of the worst feelings ever in the world. You literally feel like you're dying. You can't breathe; you writhe around like an idiot while other people try to tell you very slowly and loudly, "YOU'RE OKAY! YOU JUST GOT THE WIND KNOCKED OUT OF YOU!" It's horrible and that's exactly what happened to my son. As soon as I heard that sound, I knew I had at least thirty seconds where he couldn't do anything back.

When I was a kid I loved professional wrestling and the WWF. The one wrestler I loved most of all was Randy The

Macho Man Savage. He was the best. He was the only one with this hot manager, Jessica, who used to come out to the ring with him, and in my book that made him the coolest one of the bunch. I had always dreamed of doing what he did: circle around his downed opponent and drop an elbow on him.

I finally had my chance.

Here I was, a grown man with kids (two of whom were watching this, remember), in my front yard, pretending to be a wrestler. Neighbors had started to come out of their houses with their cell phones, cars were slowing down in the street, and I did not care. For this one moment, I was The Macho Man.

I cock-walked around my son saying, "Ooooooh, yeeeeeeah! I'm The Macho Man. Oooooooh, yeeeeeeeah!" I started tapping my elbow with my hand and nodding up and down real slow and deliberate. "Ooooooooooo, yeeeeeeah!"

"Do it, Dad! Jump on him!" one of my other kids shouted.

Then it happened. I jumped in the air with my elbow out. I leapt as high as my skinny, little Jewish legs would take me (not that high) and was laser focused on what lay beneath me. For a moment, a very brief, glorious moment, I was parallel to the ground. Weightless, if you will. I felt a strength and power that I don't ever remember feeling before or since in my life, and I looked down at my son and thought, "Not yet. The crown is not yours quite yet." Then I landed on him.

Bam!!!

And when I landed on him, I slipped a disc in my back. Nooooooooooooooo!!!!!!!!!!!!!! Can you believe that shit? Right in the middle of such a pure moment. Not only was I putting on a display for my younger kids to keep in their memory banks, not only had I re-established myself as the alpha dog to my oldest son, not only had I proved Beth wrong and showed her that I did know what I was doing, but I was finally getting a chance to be Randy The Macho Man Savage! And it was all coming to a quick and painful end.

"Get off me!" he yelled.

"Get out from under me!" I whined. I couldn't move.

When he finally got his breath back, he slid out from under me and walked into the house. There I was, alone on my front lawn with nothing but my own thoughts. Where did I go wrong? I had it planned out perfectly. Wreak mental havoc? Check. Stretch? Check. Cause him to attack carelessly? Check. I had accounted for everything...except age. At a certain point in your life, no matter how hard you train or how much you stretch out, your body can still say, "Go fuck yourself." And that's exactly what happened.

"Everything okay, Josh?"

"Go back in your house, Alan."

It just wasn't fair and as I lay there, wallowing in self-pity, I could see my front door open and feet walking toward me. I recognized those feet. They were the feet of someone who couldn't wait to come out that front door. They were the feet of someone who—and I don't have any fucking idea how she does it—had been right more times than I could even begin to count. They were the feet of someone who didn't like to gloat and by not gloating, was the biggest gloater in the history of the fucking world. They were the feet that belonged to my wife.

I was not having a good day.

She walked up to me, leaned down, and said, "On a scale of one to ten, how would you say that went?"

"I won!"

"Oh, you definitely look like a winner. That's for sure." Then she straightened up and started to walk away.

"Where are you going?" I asked. "Aren't you going to help me up?"

"Nope. Don't have time; I'm going to get a mani-pedi. If you're still there when I get back, I'll help you in." And she left.

She came back in an hour and helped me into the house. Later that day, as I was lying in bed having pretty much roofied myself with a combination of Vicodin and

Soma, my son walked into the room. He sat down in a chair and stared at me for a beat.

"I kicked your ass," he said.

"No, you didn't."

"Really? Who can't move?"

Valid point. "I kicked your ass," he said again. "Admit it."

"You did not! I threw you on the ground like a rag doll. The fight was already over when I got hurt."

He sat silent for a second. "I could kick your ass right now."

Holy shit! He was gonna pull a *Goodfellas* and smother me in my bed! Then he got up, walked to the other side of the room, put his iPad on the table, turned on the theme song from *Rocky*, and walked out the door.

He thought he was going to pull a me on *me*??!! Give me a taste of my own medicine? Did he really think that shit was going to work on me?

Damn right it was.

When the music started, I was screaming things like, "You think this is gonna bother me? I *love* this song!" and "You're gonna have to be waaaay more clever than this to bother me!" After about the fifth replay, the song was really starting to wear on me and I was saying things like, "It doesn't bother me but it's time to stop. I really need some rest because of my back. Not joking around anymore," and "Look, I said I'm done with this game, now I'm done! Do you think I can sit around here and play these games with you? Come get the iPad!" My ranting finally ended with "Beth! Beth!

Beth walked into the room and said, "What's up?"

I said, "Can you turn that off please?"

"No. Anything else?"

"No? Why not?"

"Because he told me what he was going to do, asked me if it was a good idea, and I said yes." She walked toward the door, stopped, and said, "I told you this wasn't going to end well." Then she left.

I liked it better when she didn't gloat.

Acknowledgments

I want to thank and acknowledge the following people:

My dad and mom, Thomas and Ellen Wolf. Thank you for always believing in me even when I was eating one meal a day and it was a meal I had stolen.

My brothers, Adam, Danny and Jonathan. Fuck you guys and I mean that in a loving, brotherly way.

Chelsea Handler. Pretty sure I'd be doing seven shows at the Boise Funny Bone this weekend if it wasn't for you. Thank you for letting me put my balls and stupid humor on your show. Respect isn't a big enough word...

To my friends Gavin Boyd and Joey Diaz. You guys were in the shit with me. Couldn't have made it through the Luxury Apartments without you.

My manager, Matt Van De Water. Why did you say, "You should write a book"? I hate you and love you for it at the same time. And to his mother, Katherine Van De Water, for coming up with such a classy title for the book.

Acknowledgments

My book agent, Michael Broussard. I feel cheated that you never wore your white robe to even one of our meetings. Love you. Thank you for fighting for me and this book.

My editor, Beth de Guzman. To say it was rocky for a while is like saying water is kinda wet. Thanks for seeing this through. I really appreciate all of your hard work. You believed in this book when nobody else did and for that I am forever grateful.

Tom Brunelle, Sue Murphy, Sarah Colonna, Jiffy Wild, Chris Franjola, Jen Kirkman, Heather McDonald, Fortune Feimster, Steve Marmalstein, and Dan Maurio. You guys had nothing to do with this at all. Congratulations.

Everyone at CAA who is responsible for orchestrating my "career." Thank you, thank you, thank you. Shawna, Nick, Ari, and Frank—for whatever reason you go to war for me every day and I can't thank you enough for that.

Brad Buckman, for my favorite book cover of all-time. I appreciate you finding a good shot in all of that mess. You are the king,

Everyone else at *Chelsea Lately*. You know who you are (and if you don't, I'm not talking to you); thank you for making every day a little better.

To everyone at Grand Central who had something to do with this...much love.

About the Author

Josh Wolf started doing comedy in Seattle thirteen years ago. After he moved to Los Angeles, his unique, honest, and high-energy style of storytelling made him an instant favorite at The Impov, The Laugh Factory, and The World Famous Comedy Store. He was on *Last Comic Standing* and on the season finale as one of the Last Comics Downloaded. Since then, he has had recurring acting roles in *My Name Is Earl* and has done several hosting gigs for the E! network. For two years, Josh hosted *The College Experiment*, a weekly comedic online college football show for Fox Sports. He's currently a regular on the hit E! series *Chelsea Lately* and *After Lately* and tours with Larry the Cable Guy, Chelsea Handler, and the Comedians of *Chelsea Lately*.

Ready for more of Josh Wolf's comedy?

Read his essay, *Go Lakers*, in the
#1 *New York Times* bestseller
Lies That Chelsea Handler Told Me.

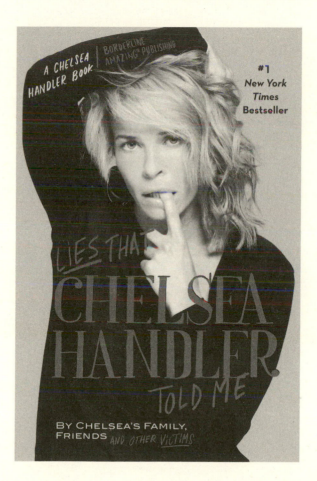